To our

Father Pat —

We love you —

Enjoy Vizena — Ojibwe

♡ Jennifer +

Benjamin

DEAD VOICES

American Indian Literature
and Critical Studies Series

Gerald Vizenor,
General Editor

Also by Gerald Vizenor

DEAD VOICES

Natural Agonies in the New World

By Gerald Vizenor

University of Oklahoma Press
Norman and London

The pictomyth on the title page is a *manidoo*; the *anishi-naabe* tribal spirit appears in creation stories, dreams, and in the voices of animals, birds, insects, trees, and those who have imagined other worlds.

The characters and human transformations in this novel arise from imagination; any resemblance to actual events is coincidental.

Text and jacket design by Cleo Patterson.

Vizenor, Gerald Robert, 1934–
      Dead voices : natural agonies in the new world / by Gerald Vizenor.
          p.   cm.—(American Indian literature and critical studies series : v. 2)
      ISBN 0-8061-2427-X (alk. paper)
      1. Indians of North America—Fiction.   I. Title. II. Series.
      PS3572.I9D43   1992
      813'.54—dc20   91-45649
                                                                        CIP

Dead Voices: Natural Agonies in the New World is Volume 2 in the American Indian Literature and Critical Studies Series.

The paper in this book meets the guidelines for permanence and durability of the Committee on Production Guidelines for Book Longevity of the Council on Library Resources, Inc. ∞

CONTENTS

DEAD VOICES

American Indian Literature
and Critical Studies Series

Gerald Vizenor,
General Editor

Possessed of nothing but my voice, the voice,
it may seem natural, once the idea of
obligation has been swallowed, that I should
interpret it as an obligation to say something. . . .
perhaps they have said me already, perhaps they
have carried me to the threshold of my story,
before the door that opens on my story, that would
surprise me, if it opens, it will be I, it will be the
silence, where I am, I don't know, I'll never know,
in the silence you don't know, you must go on, I
can't go on, I'll go on.

—Samuel Beckett, *The Unnamable*

It is hard to follow one great vision in this
world of darkness and of many changing shadows.
Among those shadows men get lost.

—John Neihardt, *Black Elk Speaks*

Write in order not simply to destroy, in order not
simply to conserve, in order not to transmit; write
in the thrall of the impossible real, that share of
disaster wherein every reality, safe and sound,
sinks. . . . There is disaster only because,
ceaselessly, it falls short of disaster. The end of
nature, the end of culture.

—Maurice Blanchot, *The Writing of the Disaster*

SHADOWS
February 1982

Bagese, as you must have heard by now, became a bear last year in the city. She is the same tribal woman who was haunted by stones and mirrors, and she warned me never to publish these stories or reveal the location of her apartment.

She was a wild bear who teased children and enchanted me with her trickster stories. She could be hesitant, the moves of an old woman, but her arms were thick, her hands were hard and wide, and she covered her mouth when she laughed because she was embarrassed that her teeth were gone.

Most of the time she celebrated her descent from the stones and the bears, wore a beaded necklace and blue moccasins that were puckered at the toes, but she would never be considered traditional, or even an urban pretender who treasured the romantic revisions of the tribal past. She was closer to stones, trickster stories, and tribal chance, than the tragedies of a vanishing race.

Bagese reeked of urine, and the marbled sweat on her stout neck had a wicked stench. She wore the same loose dress every time we met, and never washed her hair in more than a year. She was a strain on the nose, but even so she convinced me to believe in bears, and it seemed so natural at the time to hear her say that stones, animals, and birds were liberated at last in the city. She was a bear, and the bears were at war in her stories.

That bear woman warned me more than once, and with wicked humor she hauled me close to her neck and pounded me on the head with her hard hands. I felt like a mongrel, and the smell of her body made me sick to my stomach. She was a bear and teased me in mirrors as she did the children, and at the same time she said that tribal stories must be told not recorded, told to listeners but not readers, and she insisted that stories be heard through the ear not the eye. She was very determined about the ear in spite of the obvious inconsistencies. The tribal world was remembered in the ear, but she never said anything about the nose.

I listened, held my breath, and promised not

to publish what she told me. I was in her scent and could do nothing less, of course, and she told me stories about the liberation of animals, birds, and insects in the cities. She even encouraged me to tell my own stories, but my stories were lectures, or dead voices, so she told me to imagine in my own way the stories she had told me. I imitated her voice at first, practiced her hesitant manner, and repeated the sounds of her animal characters.

The secret, she told me, was not to pretend, but to see and hear the real stories behind the words, the voices of the animals in me, not the definitions of the words alone. I lectured on tribal philosophies at the university, and what she told me at first might have fallen on deaf ears in the classroom.

The best listeners were shadows, animals, birds, and humans, because their shadows once shared the same stories. She said there were tricksters in our voices and natural sounds, tricksters who remembered the scenes, the wild visions in the shadows of our words. She warned me that even the most honored lectures were dead voices, that shadows were dead in recitations. She said written words were the burial grounds of shadows. The tricksters in the word are seen in the ear not the eye.

She was such an incredible person, a natural contradiction in a cold and chemical civilization, and you will understand later why my promises were broken to remember her stories, the mirrors in her apartment, and the dead voices at the treeline. She became a bear and carved her image on a sacred copper dish the night before she vanished. She seemed to leave her mark, a signature, and that ended the game.

Bagese lived alone in a garden apartment on a busy street near Lake Merritt in Oakland, California. The front windows were below an untrimmed hedge and faced a bus stop. I visited her there many times over a period of two years. We first met on the street, and the other times were in her apartment. She wore the same clothes and never washed her hair or neck once in that time.

The city buses rattled the aluminum dishes in the sink, and overnight bits of paint and plaster were shaken loose from the ceiling and covered the table. The kitchen walls were touched with shadows of mold, the corners held their own natural traces. The ivy in a black plastic pot flourished at the windows, a lonesome brush with morning light, nothing more.

Bagese was born without a last name near a town on the crossroads at the border of the Leech Lake Reservation in Minnesota. She was born long before tribal bingo and remembered the rush of wild rice on the side of an aluminum canoe, the sound of the last cash crop in the autumn of her birth.

She learned as a child to hear the sounds of birds in their seasons. She pretended to be a bluebird, an oriole, and imitated a cardinal. Later, when she was thirteen, thin, silent, and alone, she told me she became a blue heron. She laughed when the herons mocked her moves in the cattails. She was too slow over the shiners in shallow water, and worried that she would never survive with the birds, because the birds were hunted and driven with the animals from the reservation. Their shadows were lost in lesson plans and irrefutable bird guides.

Bagese told me that she was born dead at the treeline, buried in tribal voices. I pretended to understand, but some of her stories were obscure and she never responded to my constant doubts. She was alone, silent most of the time, and never seemed to have any human friends, but she remembered too much of the natural world to ever live in isolation. At first that seemed to be a contradiction, the seclusion of her apartment and the separation of her stories about animals and birds driven to the city.

I was certain that she told no one else these stories, and that I was the only one who listened to her for more than a year. She should have been my discovery at the cages, but as you can see, she must have waited there to catch my ear. How else could she have finished her game?

Later, she convinced me that silence and isolation were learned with the eyes not the ears. She heard wild voices in the shadows, in the dance of leaves, in the pose of a cockroach on the bread board, and she remembered their stories with such pleasure, compassion, and imagination, that even a cockroach could be humbled with pride.

She remembered as a child how she turned to natural voices on the water, how she turned to nature when humans abused the silence, but more than once the loons and mallards mocked her in a canoe. She held an escape distance from the hunters and mechanical winters, practiced the manners of animals and the stories of birds. She learned to hear their shadows and survived on their stories.

I was never sure how to hear the stories she told me. I could see the scenes that she described, but meaning escaped me because the stories never ended. She just paused or stopped, and that was never certain either. She seemed to be more at ease with crows and bears than other birds and animals. There were real bears, remembered bears, bear voices, the bears in the mirrors, and the bears who returned to their shadows in the cities. She declared that the bears at last found a new wilderness in the city.

She told me the bears were tricksters in mirrors and stories in their own seasons, of course, but never more devious than humans. She was hunted with the bears by lonesome men that last autumn on the reservation. Their moves were sudden, mean, and measured in a cold and silent sight at the treeline.

Bagese remembered that one summer she was an otter on the great river, how she turned over and over in the bright water. She was an otter shadow in her stories and pretended that her coat would become a medicine bundle. She carried the sacred stones and the miigis of creation. She told me how inspired she was to give her body to the tribe, to hold that power in ceremonies, to shoot the spirit of the miigis shell that would heal the present. She said the past was stolen, the tribe was invented and recited in dead voices, and the present was hunted and driven with the animals and birds from the treelines. The animals and birds, and their shadows of creation, she insisted, had become outcasts and dreamers in the cities. She heard the dead voices and became a bear in the mirror.

Bagese Bear assumed a surname when she moved from the treeline to Oakland, California. She said her uncle had been relocated there on a federal program. Sucker, a nickname that described his mouth and the way he inhaled his words, she said, learned how to weld at a government scrapyard on San Francisco Bay. A few years later he returned to the reservation and repaired automobiles with a blowtorch. She listened and remembered his trickster stories about freedom and demons in the city. His stories were shadows and sanctuaries in the winter, and the scenes he described were new tribal creations and relocations.

Bagese has lived in that same apartment at the bus stop for more than fifteen years because it was close to the caged birds at Lake Merritt. I first met her there, at an aviary near the lake. I heard her voice in the distance, a salutation early in the morning, and there she was at a cage with the crows. She held the attention of an elder crow in a real conversation. She even had a way with the wounded golden eagle in a round cage near the crows. I mean, she spoke in such a way that the eagle answered and bounced closer to the bars to hear her stories.

My grandmother carried on with lovebirds and caged canaries, but this was different. These were wild birds caged until their wounds healed, and they listened to her stories. I mean their shadows and her stories were in the same natural time. I thought she was a shaman, but in fact she had taken me into her stories and trickster game.

I followed her to a bench at the narrow end of the lake and asked her what she had told the crows and the golden eagle. She was slow to respond to me, as if the caged birds were a secret. I did not appreciate her natural hesitation at first, but later she told stories of the wanaki trickster game in the same slow, scrupulous manner, with pauses a mean listener would take advantage of at the verbs.

I knew she had me that morning because she hesitated, covered her mouth, and then turned to the side. She seemed to laugh, but the sound was no more than sudden breath.

The folds on her neck opened and closed when she turned to the side to avoid my doubts. She would have been more cordial, it was clear, if I had been a caged bird. I mentioned the cages, what a shame it was to cage wild birds, and she turned her head in the other direction. The hesitation was more than the season.

The magnolias spread their bright shadows overnight with petals behind the bench, and the bees rushed the tender wisteria blooms that embraced the arbor near the lake.

"No shame," she whispered.

"That crow heard you."

"So he did, and so did you," she said and turned toward me. She held her hands to her mouth and looked past me, to one side of my head, and then the other.

"Can you see me here?"

"Can you hear, are you a bear?" asked Bagese.

"Hardly, but please, don't let my human appearance hold back your imagination." I moved to catch her eyes, but there was no one there. I was certain that she had bad vision.

"Your animals are dead voices."

"No, not really, my cat complains every morning, but why would you ask me about my pets?" I was suspicious and leaned back on the bench to watch her hands. She laughed, and then she rushed me on the bench and pounded me on the head. Her mouth was uncovered, close to mine for the first time, and her wild tongue bounced from side to side on her gums.

"The animals in your stories," she shouted.

"What stories?"

"The stories you hear in the mirrors," she

said and then gestured with her mouth toward the twisted wisteria bound to the arbor behind me. I turned to see the blossoms, and she was gone without a sound. I could not believe what had happened to me. I was the discoverer that morning and she turned me into a child on the bench. She tricked me and touched my sense of innocence.

Bagese has tried to lose me every time we got together, as she had done that first morning on the bench, but elusive or not, the more she hesitated and resisted my interest, the more winsome she became to me. No one ever carried on stories with caged birds the way she did, and no one could be so hard and soft at the same time, or so hesitant with such a wicked tongue. She was an old bear who teased insects with her body odor, and that was no mean distinction in the city.

I followed her that early morning to her apartment two blocks from the lake, but it was not as easy as it might sound. I never thought an old woman could trick me on the street, she could never walk that fast, but somehow she summoned two mongrels to rush me from behind, the perfect diversion. The mongrels barked, and when they retreated, she was gone.

I was certain she lived on the same block as the mongrels, and tried to imagine what she would have in the windows of her apartment. She was not behind the violets or animal figurines. I walked on both sides of the street, studied the buildings, even searched behind several homes, but there were no traces. She never told me her name.

I rested on a bench at a bus stop, and it was there, in a most unusual manner that I found her apartment. The city buses stopped at the corner, and when two students boarded they commented on the crazy bear behind the hedge. The bus roared from the curb, but there was only ivy in the window of the garden apartment. Closer, the interior came alive with mirrors, and a collection of stones, many stones, birds, leaves, flowers, insects, and other mysterious things spread out like a map on the floor. I learned later that she had laid out a wanaki game.

I crouched behind the hedge and waited at the window for a sign that she lived there. I was sure it was her apartment, but no one was there. The bright clouds of an ocean storm came ashore and rushed the eucalyptus trees. The rain came in bursts, cold and hard, and blurred the window.

Something moved in the mirrors, and the mirrors were everywhere, but the images were distant and obscure. The room was a dream scene, sensuous motions in the rain. The mirrors and stones seemed to be alive. I had no idea what the mirrors were reflecting because nothing seemed to be moving in the apartment. I would learn later, of course, that she was a bear in the mirrors, an image that escaped me for several months.

The buses roared, the windows rattled, the

storm clouds passed, and at last she appeared in the mirrors. When she saw me at the window she covered her head with her hands and danced in the leaves and stones on the floor. I could not hear, but she must have laughed over my appearance at the window, a clever ruse. I was so determined to find this woman that nothing reminded me of my compulsive and stupid behavior at the time, crouched at her kitchen window like a peeper.

She might have struck me blind, but instead she taught me how to hear and see the animals in stories. Nothing comes around in chance when the best moments are lost to manners and the clock.

"Laundry," she said at the door, and that became my nickname. She laughed and pounded me on the head. "You smell like television soap, the sweet smell of laundry is a dead voice."

Bagese invited me in, of course, and over the threshold there was a transformation of voices in the apartment, nothing in my life has ever been the same since. She told me stories with wild voices that demanded my attention and imagination, stories she warned me to remember but never, never to publish. She cursed the dead voices of civilization, the word demons who hear no stories on the run. She praised chance and tricked the demons with dead pronouns.

The wanaki chance, for instance, was her game of natural meditation, the stories that liberated shadows and the mind. Chance is an invitation to animal voices in a tribal world, and the word "wanaki" means to live somewhere in peace, a chance at peace.

She turned seven cards in the game, one each for the bear, beaver, squirrel, crow, flea, praying mantis, and the last was the trickster figure, a wild card that transformed the player into an otter, a rabbit, a crane, spider, or even a human. The animals, birds, and insects were pictured in unusual poses on the cards. The bear, for instance, was a flamenco dancer, the crow was a medical doctor, and the praying mantis was the president. The cards and creatures were stories, and she insisted that nothing was ever personal in a game of wanaki chance.

Bagese told me that the poses of the creatures were the common poses of civilization, the stories and shadows of the animals and birds in the mirrors. She compared the wanaki peace cards to tarot cards that depict the vices and virtues of human adventures, but tarot was in the eye and wanaki was in the ear. The fortunes were never the same as animal stories.

She has lived in a wanaki game since she moved to the city. Every morning she selects one of the seven cards and concentrates on the picture of the bird, animal, insect, or wild chance of the trickster. She explained that the players must use the plural pronoun *we* to share in the stories and become the creatures on the cards. That morning she had become the stories of the crow and gathered bits and pieces of nature, fallen leaves and feathers near the lake, and placed them in similar positions in her apartment, which was all part of the wanaki chance. The shape of the lake was obvious once she told me about the game. The objects were laid out as she had found them in the miniature shape of Lake Merritt.

The beaver and squirrel stones were placed in the north on the floor of her apartment, the bear in the east, the flea in the west, the crow and praying mantis in the south, and the last card was the trickster in the center of the wanaki game.

I was more than eager to remind her that the wanaki cards were an obvious contradiction to what she had told me. The pictures on the cards were the same as written words and could not be heard. I was certain she wanted me to ask obvious questions. "So, how can you hear stones and pictures?"

"The bear is painted not printed, and the praying mantis is seen as the president, this is a shadow, a chance not a word," she insisted.

"Written words are pictures."

"Printed books are the habits of dead voices," she said and turned a mirror in my direction to distract me. "The ear not the eye sees the stories."

"And the eye hears the stories."

"The voices are dead."

"So, the wanaki pictures are dead."

"There are no others, these are my picture stories, no one sees them but hears my stories," she said and then drew one of the seven cards in the game. She held the picture to the mirror and the praying mantis became a bear.

The natural meditation scene was conspicuous, and the dead birds on the miniature bay were a bit much, but she enlivened my ambivalence with stories about a tribal woman who brought dead animals and birds back to life on the reservation.

"She must have been the resurrection shaman."

"You could say that," she responded.

"She could make a fortune at a chemical company."

"She already has on weekends," said Bagese.

"So, why are you playing miniature meditation with leaves and twigs in your apartment when you could bring back the dead and buy your own reservation?"

I never doubted that she had the power and the stories to bring back the dead, even dead voices at a great distance. The moment she appeared as a bear was more than enough power to transform the world, at least in my mind, but the mirrors that haunted her apartment were too much for me to understand.

The return of dead animals and birds was a story that made sense, but the mirrors that haunted her apartment were outside of my imagination and appreciation. These mirrors held images that were never in that room, and there were images that she could see, but not me. I avoided the mirrors for fear that my face would vanish, or that my image would tell me who the animals were in my past. My present memories and insecurities were more than enough for me to understand. The evolution of the animals in me, or as she said, the animal shadows that came to me as stories, would be too much to endure at rush hour, in line at the bank, or in a lecture at the university.

I was not surprised to learn that there seemed to be a hierarchy of mirrors in that apartment. There were round hand mirrors everywhere, beveled mirrors, suspended mirrors, table mirrors, tile mirrors, and framed mirrors covered the walls. She teased me to watch myself in the mirrors, the smaller mirrors. She even positioned a portable mirror to catch me when I sat at the kitchen table. When I refused to look into the mirrors she laughed and pounded me on the head.

I can never be sure, but there seemed to be something sexual about the mirrors in her apartment. There was never any doubt that her lust almost did me in when at last, after seven months of visits, she appeared to me as a bear in the tabernacle mirror. I will never forget that moment in her maw, and since then she has never pounded me on the head.

The Empire tabernacle mirror was mounted with distinction on a partition just inside the door to her apartment. As the door opened, there was the tabernacle. The distinctive decorated glass was the first mirror in her apartment. I have never seen anything like it, not to mention the haunting reflections of the other mirrors. The tabernacle frame was turned and painted black and gold with carved rosettes in the corner blocks. The upper part of the framed mirror was decorated with the creatures pictured on the wanaki cards. The face of the trickster, a bear in a human figure at the center of the scene, was a miniature metallic mirror. I saw her as a bear in that tabernacle mirror. The landscape was painted on the reverse side of the glass, and the main mirror was below the wanaki scene.

Bagese told me stories in the animal, bird, and insect voices of the wanaki game. She teased the trickster in the tabernacle, and pounded the mirrors that leaned too close to the dead voices. Two years later she was gone without a trace. The mirrors were down, the apartment was empty, but the ivy held to the window. I remember her stories as our stories now, and if she hears them told once more, even these published versions, she might return to pound me on the head as she promised.

STONES
December 1978

These stories are about the unusual creation of this earth, wind and stones, and our pleasures with tricksters at night in the cities. These stories are about the first humans, an old woman, her daughter, and three grandsons who once lived in their own trickster stories.

Look around you now at the mountains and the meadows, the lakes and rivers. Outside there are trees and flowers, birds, bears, and insects, but the old woman and her daughter in these creation stories lived at a time when the earth was covered with low brush, nothing more, not even stones, or the wild sound of human words. There were no birds or spiders at that time, no crows or praying mantis.

One summer the daughter was out searching for something to eat in an open field. She found some berries and picked them to eat right there. She remembered that place and returned there often to gather the sweet berries for her mother.

Later, when she was picking more berries on a hot afternoon, she heard a noise that sounded like a breath of wind, a wild wind. The wind was from the west, down from the blue mountains, and the wind was in love with the young woman who picked berries. She was alone and the wind wanted to love her right there in the field of berries.

She turned and saw the wind coming over the field but there was nothing she could do to stop the wind from the mountains. She tried to distract the wind as best she could, but there were no bushes to hide behind, so she stood her ground in the berries.

There was no one but her mother to call for protection, so she leaned toward the west wind and held her dress down with both hands. The wind was very firm and lifted the back of her dress, and then more and more on the sides. She struggled to hold the back and sides down but the wind lifted the dress and she could not pull it down again for some time, not until the wind had passed and the fields were quiet again. She returned to picking berries and thought nothing about the time the west wind raised her dress on that hot afternoon.

The old woman had a peculiar feeling about her daughter, she sensed that something had happened while her daughter was out picking berries. She watched her daughter move and wondered if she had been touched by the spirits.

"Do you ever see others when you are out picking berries in the field?" the old woman asked her daughter. She turned to one side and pretended not to be so interested in the answer.

"Never," said the daughter.

"Something is wrong then," said the old woman. She asked again but her daughter insisted that she never saw anyone when she was picking berries or at any other time.

Later, the daughter began to wonder if there was something wrong with her, but she could not remember much more from that time she picked berries, nothing more than the wind on that hot summer afternoon.

She told her mother about the wild wind that had raised her dress and the old woman knew at once what had happened. She waved her arms at the wind in the four directions, and then looked toward the sun.

"The sun, it was the sun," said the old woman.

"The wind was under my dress," said the daughter. Some time later she gave birth to three children, the first crossblood tricksters on the earth, and the earth would never be the same.

The new mother held the first child in her arms, the first manidoo or spirit of this earth.

The manidoo was named Naanabozho and he appeared at birth to be a normal child. She was very happy and then she heard a voice from the mountains, the west wind told her to place the child on the earth. She held Naanabozho and would not listen to the wind, and that was that. The wind told her once more to put the child down, but she held the child who would be a trickster close in her arms.

"There, too late," said the west wind. "If you had put your child down on the earth when you were told to, the child would have been able to walk like an animal, but now it will take about a year before he can learn to walk."

Children would have walked like animals, like a bear, at birth, but because she would not put her child down when the wind told her to do so, it now takes children much longer to learn how to walk as a human on two feet.

Soon her second child was born, a manidoo child with some human features, but he was not the same as the first trickster child. Remember, these were the first tricksters and manidoo children on the earth, a time when there were no stones, animals, birds, trees, or flowers.

The third manidoo child did not appear to be human in any sense of the word. The last born trickster was a stone, a hard stone. With the birth of the stone there were birds and animals, flowers and insects on the earth. A bear, a bird, a stone could feel at home on the earth for the first time.

Naanabozho, the first born manidoo, who had become a trickster spirit, was much too eager to hunt and kill what he could find, even the first little birds in their nests. Like a domestic animal he brought what he had killed to show to his mother. She told him never to kill little birds again. Naanabozho did not listen, and he did not stop killing little spirits on the earth. He was a trickster child.

Stone, the last born manidoo, seldom moved from his place on the earth. The birds, flowers, and animals came with his birth. Naanabozho and his other brother were together most of the time, but not with their brother Stone. At night the brothers shared their adventures with Stone because he could not travel.

Naanabozho was bothered that his travels and adventures were limited by his mother to the time it would take him to return to his brother Stone, so he asked his other brother if he could kill Stone.

Naanabozho listened for a time, but his brother was silent. He never answered the question. So, the first born manidoo child on the earth decided to listen to himself and planned to kill his brother Stone. This would be the first and most terrible crime on the earth, the death of the first born stone.

The trickster borrowed an axe from his grandmother and used it to kill his brother Stone but the axe broke in two places. Stone was hard and could not be killed with an axe.

Then Naanabozho asked his brother Stone how to kill him.

"I will do whatever you tell me to do to kill you."

"Build a fire," said the manidoo trickster Stone. "Put me in the fire and when my body is red hot then throw cold water on me and watch what will happen to me."

Naanabozho built a huge fire. He threw more wood on the fire as his brother Stone instructed him to do from the very heart of the fire, and then the trickster waited until his brother was red hot in the coals.

"Are you hot enough, is it time now?"

"No, not yet," said Stone.

"Wait, wait, more fire, is it time now?"

"Yes, it is the time," said Stone.

"Here comes the cold water then," said Naanabozho as he poured the water on his brother Stone. Stone was red hot and cracked in several places when the cold water touched him, and then he broke into thousands and thousands of pieces and flew in the four directions of the earth. At first it seemed that one of the first manidoo children had died on the earth, that the first stone had come to a wild death in a fire.

Naanabozho believed that he had killed Stone. The distance he could travel would never be limited by his brother. He could travel great distances at night and not bother to return to his brother, but Stone had outwitted his brother the trickster, the one who liked to kill.

Stone had broken into several families and covered the earth in the four directions. Stone families lived everywhere, in the mountains, on the rivers, in the meadows, in the desert. No matter where that trickster traveled he would not be far from his brother and the families of the stone. One break of the stone became a bear in the cities. Stone is in a medicine pouch. Stone is in the mirror.

Stone created the world of nature and the wanaki cards, and taught the tribes how to meditate. He created three sets of seven cards with pictures of animals, birds, insects, and the picture of his brother the trickster on one card in each set.

Naanabozho heard that his picture was on the cards so he buried two of the sets. He was tired and bored so one set of the cards survived. The third set of wanaki cards has been used to teach the tribes to remember stories and to meditate. The players create their own cards, but the seven must picture the bear, beaver, squirrel, crow, flea, praying mantis, and the trickster.

The player arises at dawn, turns one of the seven cards, meditates on the picture, and imagines he has become the animal, bird, or insect on the card for the day. Then stories are told about the picture and the plural pronoun *we* is used to be sure nature is not separated from humans and the wanaki game.

Stone created a meditation that would never leave him out. He taught that on each day a card is selected the player walks on a familiar trail and gathers fallen leaves, flowers, feathers, and other natural things of the season. Then he meditates on these things and places them in a room or on a table according to where they were found on the trail.

When animals, birds, insects, and living things are seen on the trail a stone is placed to remember the place. In this way, Stone is always present where life would be in the wanaki game.

The game goes on for seven days, a new picture and identity at dawn. The last card in the game is the picture of the trickster. The last card leaves the choice of identities to the player, an imaginative picture for the last day of the game. Many players become eagles, and cranes, some become beavers and other water animals, and others become beautiful birds on the last card of the wanaki game.

Stone created a game that remembers him in stories. To end the game his brother would have to end the world, and he would never do that because he would be too bored and lonesome. Stone became a bear in his own trickster meditation. The wanaki game is his war with loneliness and with human separations from the natural world.

BEARS
March 1979

Turn the first card at dawn.

Bears in the wanaki circle, bears in the east.

The bears are with me now on this first turn of the cards. The stones are broken into bears and land in the east. We are the bears of chance, bears turned over on the mountain wind, turned over on the cards. We are bears on that slow burn at dawn, down from the wild treelines to our tribal agonies in the cities.

We are bears in the rain this morning, the picture of the bear and the bear in the mirror. We are more than a word, more than a word beast, we are remembered in stories. We return to the heart in stories, a return to nature in the pictures of the wanaki cards. We are bears on the rise in the cities this morning. The wordies held our name in isolation, even caged us on the page. We are bears not cold separations in the wilderness of dead voices.

We are together at dawn. No other bears are on the same trail around the lake. The caged eagle and the crows hear our stories, but the wordies would think we were strange at this hour, talking out loud to the crows in plural pronouns. Not many wordies would see me as the bear, and that is how bears have survived the hunters and the tourists. They might wonder who is with me, but few would see the real me in our stories.

Someone hears us with the crows at the cage, a fresh wordy in loose clothes, and he reeks of perfume and laundry soap. Even the crows move back, out of his poison scent. How can we remember who the wordies are when they smell the same, as if they came from the same box of soap. Their animals are lost, and no one can hear the stories in their blood.

The laundry boy follows us to the bench near the wisteria. His mouth moves with dead voices. How can he be so young and so dead? How could he kill all the animals and birds in his heart? How can he go on? He has no stories to remember because he asks us about our stories. He must be a trickster who played so hard he killed the animals in his own heart.

Laundry must think we are separated, he must think he understands our loneliness at this hour, but he is so easy to distract with the obvious in the natural world. Had he taken the scent of magnolia we might have heard his voice.

We crisscrossed the street and he was sure to follow that morning, so we turn to the right and circle around, but he continued on our trail. The mongrels were roused by the bear and shied by our shadows. The laundry boy lurched at the words and the mongrels barked him down to the animals in his heart. Too bad, he turned to the darkness not the treeline, and the mongrels sensed that he holds back the light in his own stories. The wordies close their books at the first bark and lose their way without a sentence.

Laundry believes he discovers people on the street, as if he landed as some pioneer of tribal stories, but he got lost in his own wilderness of words. How could he hear our stories? He never had his own stories to remember.

Laundry sees the darkness behind his eyes and waits to discover the last words that might hold back his death. How does he go on without stories? He comes so clean to the cage and dies over words in a dream.

We are seen as circus bears under a clear umbrella. We can jump rope to the crack of a whip and ride a small motorcycle in a tight circle on the sawdust. We are bears with an audience, bears in the word, and we are alone at night in a chemical civilization.

Some wordies laugh at us from their windows on the block. Children reach out at a great distance in their dreams to touch our nose, to hide in our maw, and pull our thick hair high around their thin necks in winter.

There, at that clean pink house with the wild shutters, a thin woman leans over the fence as we pass. We were invited to touch her high breasts, the breasts steam in the cold rain. She was silent and never moved. Would she be worried that we were bears?

Laundry cursed the mongrels, and we were alone under the umbrella. We were alone with our pronouns and stories, and there were distances even in our pictures. We might have been a mourning dove, or an otter on the great river. We are bears this morning, and later the cards might turn us into birds at dawn. We could be cockroaches, and we are tricksters in the end. The cards protect us from the dead voices of the wordies.

Broken windows on a truck.

Beer cans and chicken cartons at the bus stop. Cigarettes buried in the concrete.

Printed flowers on a wet scarf distract us from the trees and flowers behind the building. There, spread like a sacred shield over the wire near the storm sewer, the wet red flowers and leaves on the scarf seem more real than the trumpet vines that decorated the center of the cedar trees across the barrier.

The cedars were moist and gentle in the rain, but the cotton flowers bound a culture that made more sense in the cities. So, we were circus bears with a bright silk scarf. First we smelled it, our nostrils flared over the neck perfume of a hesitant blonde, a teacher at the public school. She left a scent of beer and beans, garlic, chalk, and she takes her place in our memories.

We heard more than stories of trees and flowers, so we hounded the material world on the block. We brushed a fence woven with bamboo, pounded a rock garden, and touched an iron bird over a mailbox, and we laid our paws on houses, window frames, fences, and golden doors. The colors of paint were brighter than the flowers at one house.

The garden hoses were silent in the rain. The rattlers waited at the head of the coil. That blue hose became an urban night chant near the cedar trees. The music became weaker and died on the wet lawn. The plastic hose raised the wind, and the demons rushed the hollows. The sound was wild, a scream near the treeline, and then the hunters were touched with their own poisons.

We were bears and marched back to our apartment. We should have been worried about domestic animals, but we were wet and so close to home. At the back of one of the best laid gardens we were warned not to enter. Even the hose was coiled and covered.

The sign was painted in bright orange letters, "beware of the guard dogs." We admired the tailored trees, the rich flowers, succulents, ferns and vines, but stay behind the fence. Bears have no fear. The warning was lost, because we had no fear of mongrels.

Laundry was barked down by the mongrels, but clean wordies are not bears. We brushed the iron gate and teased the tense mongrels. The scent of bear had been in the air since dawn. They were trained to declare war over the boundaries of the garden, and war it would be for the blossoms that morning. In waves the beasts barked and pushed at the gate. We were bears and had stones, the natural world, and the best stories on our side. The mongrels had their master, the chemical remains of nature, and the garden of names on their side.

Reservation mongrels roam at a distance to avoid bears, but these beasts had docked tails and pressed their noses on the iron fence. We heard their stories once. Their ancestors would have courted the wind and circled the boundaries of an escape distance. These mongrels were fascists trained to die for stunted trees and succulents. They have no choices in the world, no pictures, stones, no stories to turn the seasons. They were mongrels in the bark, nothing more.

We decided not to enter the garden. Instead, we pissed at the corner post behind a bush to tease the master and his mongrels with our scent. They were crazy, the three of them barked and shouted, and the master threw open the gate even before our dress was down. We roared and thrust the umbrella at them, but one leaped on the plastic, and the other one tore our dress. We beat around the corner and escaped.

The bears were out that morning to hear the

other animals, but those demons in the garden became wordies in the garden. They were ready to hear the rattle and scorn of the evil gambler of the mountains. What will become of the mongrels with no stories?

The miniatures that bark in the windows would never cross the threshold to menace bears. They bark with big hearts in small bodies, and they remember great stories.

When two doors slammed shut we hurried around the corner past the houses. There at the corner, the tender magnolia blossoms, beaten in the rain, seemed to reach out to us with a personal invitation to the season. The petals blushed and dropped as we listened. Even the apartment building across the street told stories. A sign on the door declared that the building was not tied to the earth and had not satisfied earthquake construction standards.

Laundry was at the window, cold, clean, and lonesome, when we returned to our apartment. That pathetic boy lost his way on a word map. The wordies at the windows want to come in, mongrels want to get out, so one must imagine that the others are freer. The bears hear the best stories at common thresholds, but wordies know nothing about bears. Laundry knows nothing but dead voices.

You see, he heard nothing in the tabernacle mirror, not even his own stories. He heard nothing in our stones and pictures, and asked the same stupid question over and over again, "what does this mean, what does that mean?" We pounded him on the head as much as we could to loosen his brain so he could hear the tricksters and the bears.

One summer we were captured and caged behind a restaurant at a resort. The cage was nothing more than chicken wire, and the plastic cover leaked, but we danced in the hard rain. The rain came down to be with us, and we were free from tourists in wet weather. In fair weather, thousands of curious and cautious wordies parked their cars close to the cage for protection. Children threw stones and marbles at us through the wire. Once or twice an innocent child would include us in a ball game. Parents, but never the children, were surprised when we threw the ball back. For this we were given the remains of picnic lunches, hamburger buns, cheese, the last bread, but never meat.

We roamed until dark in tight circles, bears at the treeline in a chicken cage. We were hosed down with the concrete at night. When autumn came, and the last tourists returned home, we overturned the wire and escaped to the cities.

That blue hose is stuck in our memories, a desert rattler on the first morning out as bears. No one can hold down our stories, but even so, we were dominated by a television screen near the bakery at the end of the block. The monitor was mounted over a counter in a commercial loan office, and the camera scanned the entrance to the building.

The Academy Loans words were burned on the screen, and the guard at the door could have been another garden mongrel, but that never held back the bears. We saw ourselves on screen as invitations to the loan games, disguised as miniature wordies.

We were bears at the entrance, dead voices on the television screen, but how could we resist our own picture? That's when we understood our distance, how our stories were separated by the games on television. The screen was surprised that we were there. We remember our own pictures and stories. On the monitor our face was a shadow, blurred when we moved, and thick dark hair covered our neck and ears. We pressed our nose wide on the window at the entrance, and our face was pale, human, flattened out on television. We ducked at the window and became wordies on television. We might have lost our stories with a loan.

The name of the loan business was shown in reverse below our head on the screen. The children remembered that name backward and rushed to our side, to be seen and separated on the screen.

Even our bear stories were burdened with the material world. The men who once hunted bear invented properties and possessions and made reservations for the tribes so their women could hang their clothes out to dry on the line without fear.

The hunters wanted and wasted their stories. The wordies inherited dead voices and lost the stories that held their world together. The hunters were behind the weak pictures on that monitor, behind the loans, sewing machines, metal bundles, engines, and steering wheels. We moved on the screen and our picture came closer to their machines than we had ever been in the city.

On the other side of the street we heard the salmon streams and the end of our hibernation. The silk scarf, the bright blue hose, the television screen, and the pictures on the cards turned us back to meditation and the mirrors. Television stole the shadows of the wordies and the mirrors held our stories.

We never had any trouble remembering to use plural pronouns, but most wordies could not understand who we were talking about. They saw the old woman but not the bear. We are one and the same. There's a trickster in the use of words that includes the natural world, a world according to the we, and the we is our metaphor in the wanaki game.

The second walk as bears was even more interesting than the first move at dawn. We stayed clear of television and material scenes, the hose and scarf were out, and we tried to avoid the trash on the streets. Anyway, bears were never known for their tidy nests.

Laundry was so clean he could have lost his hands. We told him that the only clean place we ever lived was in a mirror. He believed everything we told him, but it still took him ages to see us in the mirror. That boy washed his hands too much after play.

On our first walk we paid too much attention to mongrels and the way people dump their ideas and trash on the street. We struggled to hear the flowers over the trash, but even then we were at the trash of the natural world, the torn petals, fallen blossoms, feathers, and more, that we gathered and placed in our apartment. The more we held to flowers and leaves, the less cultural trash we noticed near the lake.

We tried not to tease the mongrels, but how else could we raise the remains of nature in the wanaki game? Our mere scent left a trail of barking mongrels on the block, and sometimes people thought we had criminal intentions. Can you imagine a real crime under the magnolias? Maybe there were wordies who practiced harmless abusement in the acacia?

Our first light pounded on the clouds, the last touch of night in the mirrors. Mourning doves whistled on the wires. We were alone once more on the streets at dawn, and saw those lonesome faces behind the window blinds, wordies waiting in fear that the world might have changed overnight. They waited for an earthquake, the last rain, their stories to shout from the shadows, and never seemed to sleep. What did they think about a bear in a print dress who stopped to admire the overnight trails of snails on the sidewalk? Could they see our faces in the rain pools?

Mourning doves hold the earth to the wire. City birds pose in a line, but not the eagles, or crows. The wordies wait in lines, but not bears, eagles, crows. We are bears and we roar under the wire. How many wordies mourn on the wire, and how many wordies have become bears?

Camellias lean over the concrete. We remember in our stories, but bears never learned the names of flowers. We hear the scent with a natural touch, the scent that was heard by our ancestors. There are no stories to remember in laundry perfume, only the crack of dead voices in a chemical civilization. How is it possible to come closer to flowers with discovered names? Could the hunter learn to shout the names of the bear, panther, and lion, rather than shoot them? No, the hunter is a saboteur, he deceives the heart and shoots from a great distance without a name or stories. To down a hunter how would we shout his name? To the silence in the stones?

Laundry comes closer with a name, but no stories are heard in his scent. Throw his clean clothes over the wire and the doves would never return to mourn the bears. The camellias, acacia, wisteria, and the wild plums are in bloom at the lake. Closer to our apartment we are overcome by the exhaust of laundries.

We brush on the cedars and pinch their berries. We are bears on our second trail in the wanaki game, and we have nothing to fear but hunters and the police. We remember the world with stories that wordies would rush to discover, hunt, and capture in a name. The hunters pretend to own the world with names. We are bears with the last pronouns down from the treelines in mountains. You can hear the roar of nature in our stories at dawn in the city.

The wanaki is cedar bark, thick oak leaves, dove feathers, camellias, and plum blossoms patched on the floor of our apartment. On the other side of the miniature lake wisteria, bay leaves, narrow red petals, and seven stones to remember the birds on the trail. Later that month at dusk we circled the lake once more, and with ceremonial care returned the blossoms, leaves, and feathers, to the places they were found. The stones were laid our as memories in the apartment.

That coil of blue hose had vanished.

The mongrels barked at a calico cat on the iron gate. The windows were clouded.

Overnight the hard rain brought down the plum blossoms and covered our shoulders. We browsed in the cedar and chewed bark. The miniatures on leashes were worried over the scent of bears near our garden apartment. Laundry learned their names and put them at ease.

We turned the first card at dawn and we were bears.

 # FLEAS
May 1979

Turn the second card at dawn.

Fleas in the wanaki circle, fleas in the west.

The fleas are with me now on this second turn of the cards. The stones are broken into fleas and land in the west. We are the fleas of chance, fleas turned over on the mountain wind, turned over on the cards. We are fleas on that slow burn at dawn, down from the wild treelines to our tribal agonies in the cities.

We are fleas buried in a mansion of hair and tender heat. We beat the crown and mount the dawn in slow leaps on the back of bears, doves, crows, and mongrels, and our stories honor sand and circus blankets.

The scent of moist eucalyptus is on the rise,

and the trees waver on the water. The trees hold the last reins of the sun over the lake, and the light breaks on the windows of the buildings downtown.

Seven ducks circle overhead and land on the lake as we start on the trail with the fleas. The shadows are moist in the gardens, and we ride on the back of a mongrel down the fenceline. There must be someone at home, the lonesome statues lean that way over the roses. We must brush their elbows, wet and blue, and no one told them their moves were at home in the west.

We are fleas on the trail at dawn. The trees and poles near the lake are as straight as the hair on the shoulders of a bear. Our bodies are hard, but even the sparrows could crunch us down in a single thrust. So, we ride on the neck of a sparrow in our stories, mock our natural enemies, and suck just enough blood not to crash land.

Hundreds of birds are on the wires. Two mourning doves bounce their heads and then whistle down to the grass, out of sight. The stout robins flick their tail feathers in the sun, worried on the wire. Our distant relatives ride the doves and robins. Later, we hear the sound of a peacock on the other side of the lake.

Last night, before we became fleas with the turn of the wanaki card in the west, we told stories about fleas. Our apartment had been taken over by fleas, not just the fleas in the game,

but hordes of other fleas, hundreds of generations of fleas told their stories in the building.

The other tenants were worried about insect
infestation, so the owner hired an exterminator
who landed in uniform with tanks and hoses. He
learned the common habits of fleas and considered them the enemies of health and wealth in
the city. We studied his habits, the chemicals he
used to burn time, and decided that he was a
demon who would overturn our inheritance as
fleas, so we declared him the primal enemy of
life.

He recited the diseases that fleas could
cause, such as typhus and bubonic plague, but
the fear of fleas he spread became the survival of
the exterminator in a chemical civilization. His
poison was worse than our bite or the diseases
he blamed on the fleas.

For months the tenants had counted their
flea bites like war wounds, but the exterminator
was not allowed to poison our apartment. Naturally, the fleas abandoned the rest of the building
and told their stories of survival in our apartment.

The we is me and the fleas, and the bear in
the mirror. We were never able to catch fleas,
birds are much faster than bears. Once or twice
we pinched them, but when we opened our fingers the flea leaped into hair and told her escape
stories in the blood. We became the adventures
and close encounters in the memories of that flea.

We teased our natural enemies in the world

to remember our stories. With the turn of the card we grazed as fleas in the eucalyptus groves near the campus. Fleas, we were told, hated the scent of the tree. We gathered the hard flower crowns and aromatic leaves and spread them around the apartment, in the corners, under the boards and cushions.

Families of fleas were driven from their sanctuaries overnight, their sources of food were tainted by the scent, and there was a real crisis in who was a real flea in the world of our apartment. Our blood was in their stories, we had brought the hated eucalyptus into their lives and upset thousands of flea families who were already worried about the exterminator. With that hated scent the fleas remembered the worst in the chemical wars against them.

Hawk, the oldest flea in the building, worried about their children and how they would survive the poisons in the blood of humans. The birds were poisoned to the bone, bears to the wild heart. Would the fleas be driven from the apartment and the world with chemical weapons, aromatic leaves, pet collars, and other devices?

The elders ruled that we were tricksters in a wicked world, in a world of dead voices, poisoned by the wordies who would never hear their stories in the blood. The fleas were determined to hold their last apartment in the building. That scent of eucalyptus inspired a new consciousness and a counter movement to overcome fear and reclaim the bodies of the bears, doves, and other stories in the blood.

"No one has the right to poison our families," said Hawk. He leaped higher and higher the way fleas do when they lecture, and he was better than most at his advanced age. "Our families have been here for many generations, much longer than the eucalyptus, and we have rights to the animals and birds on the block."

Market, the trickster who tried to overcome the scent of eucalyptus, told the flea families that rights come not with manners but with power and violence. She became the natural teacher of flea survival. She learned from the cockroaches that a little bit of poison is the best defense in the chemical world. "We must arm ourselves with poison, remember our stories in the blood, and fight for what is ours, the right to mount, ride, and suck on bird and beast is aboriginal."

"The exterminator hears no aboriginal rights," said Hawk.

"The bodies we trust have been denied by chemical demons, but we will never live in fear or disgrace," said Market. "We are proud fleas and we must attack the exterminator at dawn with his own poison."

The fleas gathered on a cushion under the window in our apartment. We listened to the flea lectures on the conditions of war late into the night. The owner would give the exterminator permission in the morning to poison the last apartment in the building, in one massive attack.

What could be done to save the fleas from chemical genocide?

Market had a scheme and invited the fleas from other families on the block to the war council that night. The fleas had never shared their political or chemical enemies in the past, and there was no reason to believe that an exterminator in one building would obligate other fleas to a war.

The dove fleas were dedicated to peace. The fleas who rode on the garden mongrels and the sparrows supported the war proposal. The bear fleas were neutral but agreed to summon the birds on the wire to attack the exterminator.

The crows menaced the other birds to celebrate and defend the rights of insects. The grosbeaks waited in the bush to hear more, and the cardinals were the last to support the war. The fleas lectured and argued for hours on the cushion. The birds would attack the exterminator from every direction in the morning. Even the wrens agreed, but the doves and their fleas said they would remain on the wire and pray for peace.

"Who are these mourning fleas?" asked Hawk.

"They think doves are the most civilized," said Market.

"Mother earth on a wire," said Hawk.

"The fleas that would become doves and fly."

"Fleas on a wire are no better than a circus," said Hawk.

"We heard that," said a polished dove flea. Conn was perched on the window lock high above the cushion. "We choose peace not war, because nothing of value has ever been gained through violence."

"High wire circus fleas, nothing more," said Hawk.

"We raise no conditions that our ride with the doves is any better than the ride to a dump on the back of a bear, or the crack of a crow on the road," said Conn.

"The condition is extermination," shouted Hawk.

"Peace is meditation, not a compromise with power," said Conn.

"The circus is peace," said Hawk.

"My father was a performer in a flea circus," said Conn.

"This is our last circus, we are in our last apartment, the wires are down, and peace means nothing to the exterminator, not even a good story over lunch," said Hawk.

"There is the smell of evil in the air, and this is not the first time that evil has entered our lives," said Market. "Some time ago several younger fleas, and you know who you are, were tricked to ride on the back of a cat that turned out to be a mechanical pet operated by the exterminator, and you should remember, the dove fleas sounded the warning and saved your lives."

We decided on war, war with the exterminator in the morning, and then we told stories in the blood the rest of the night. There were no lights or blood in the land of evil, and the fleas were no more than bad dreams on the backs of vicious beasts. The first fleas were cursed to ride on demons, and the demons sucked the sun from the sky and the fire from the sea. The rest of the earth was dark, we were told.

The ancient fleas were innocent and backward. They knew nothing about the blood of beasts, and moved from hand to mouth without visions, one demon to another when the flesh turned cold.

The first fleas had no culture, no literature, no cushions, no circus, no birds on the wire or bears to ride home. They did little more in ancient times than bite and flee the darkness.

Then we heard the deliverance stories of the fleas, our transformation on the back of the first wild cat. The great flea bearer took us on and delivered us to human bodies.

The flea families were silent on the cushion as our origin stories were told. Even the children turned from their beast games to listen. The stories in the blood had been told so many times from hair and cushions that most fleas heard their own versions, and the best flea stories include experiences of the present.

The grateful cat, our great flea bearer from the time of the demons, gathered our ancestors, the first flea families, on her back in the dense hair between her shoulders. But when the grateful cat tried to leave the land of fire eaters, the demons breathed flames on her body. The fleas scurried down her back between the burning hairs and hid in the last of the fur under her tail, near her asshole.

The grateful cat wandered for many nights without food or water, from shelter to shelter, over blue mountains and through the brush. She told stories about the strange beasts she encountered on the earth. Our ancestors rode close to her hot asshole, because her body was blotched with burned flesh and hair. From time to time wild fleas from other families would bite the great flea bearer and she became so angry she ate them. Our families were wise enough never to bite the cat that carried them. Our ancestors were on a mythic ride to paradise near the asshole of the great flea bearer.

Hunger was a common experience in our ancient flea families. Some of our ancestors were so weak with hunger that they lost their grip in the hair around the asshole, dropped to the ground and died in strange places without blood. Others were so hungry they were tempted to bite the cat that carried them, but such thoughts were terminal. Sudden death came to those who were stupid enough to bite the great flea bearer. One bite and our first families would have lost their chance for salvation and civilization. The asshole of the great cat was the best our ancestors could do at the time.

The grateful cat delivered us to the warm naked bodies of humans, and we learned to live with them for many generations. The great bearer sat down close to the humans, and as she purred our relatives leaped from her asshole onto the humans. That night the ancient families held their first feast on human blood. Our ancestors took their first bites on humans and we became many on the stories in their blood.

Fleas need stories in the blood, but never seem to need solace. That night we waited in silence for the stories to continue in the apartment. The stories turned morose the closer we came to the hour of our war with the exterminator. Some fleas were asleep on the cushion, and others stretched their legs and remembered their best beasts and birds, their rides and stories in the blood. The mirrors in the apartment held the bears, but no one tried to leap through that escape distance.

"Your thigh alone could feed many families for who knows how long," said a stout heroic flea. Frog cleared his huge sucker and watched our every move. He was not the only one who wanted a bite of the huge fleas. We were more than anyone had ever seen, but we were secure because fleas had never turned to cannibalism.

"Until now," said Frog.

"Until now, what?"

"Until now we've never taken a bite of our own."

"Until now you've never been cursed," we said and bushed him with eucalyptus leaves. Frog retreated to the window and pleaded for forgiveness and humor. The others fleas shouted he was a lecherous coward. "The blood of giants is poison to the little cannibals."

"No, you're not poison," said Frog.

"You need another ride near an asshole, near an asshole," we told him and inspired the other fleas to chant the same. "You can lead the attack in the morning and take the first bite of the exterminator."

"This flea has no fear," said Frog.

"Our bearer, the grateful cat would have it no other way," said Market. "She would have us learn how to ride near an asshole again and again on the trail to the city without taking a bite."

"Romantic heretics," said Frog.

"The grateful cat taught the fleas how to survive, a lesson that was lost on you," said Hawk. "Our ancestors had enough sense not to attack the asshole that gave them reason and a free ride."

We are fleas on a meadow and ride down to the lake on the back of a raccoon. The lake is our retreat, and the beasts who carried our ancestors past the demons came to the city with their stories. The exterminator never heard the real world that died with his poisons. He was secure in chemical names, but lost the words that ended in sanctuaries.

The willows leaned over the benches. The birds carried our stories to the heather and rose, the bottle brush, and orange trees in bloom on the boulevard. At the corner a child asked her mother who we were, and we were fleas with a selection of the natural world in our wanaki game.

"What does that old woman look for?"

"Trees, birds, loose change, and things."

"We are fleas," we insisted with humor. "Fleas out for our morning walk after the rain, spring fleas waiting to catch a ride with a cat, and are you the cat?"

"Not a cat, the cats stay home," said the child.

"Then you must be the bird we heard."

"She said a bird," the child said to her mother and reached for her hand. The mother was worried that we were fleas, bothered by our words not our clothes or manners.

"Wild words raise the wild in the pictures," we told the mother and reached to touch the child. The mother hurried her child around the corner to avoid the fleas.

They would have been much happier if we had been domestic, some miniature on a leash. The trees and bushes reached out to take us in at the corner. Some people worry more about fleas than they do earthquakes or the demons who would end our stories in the blood.

The other gardens on the block posed, the blossoms saluted in the right direction. We were circus fleas and there on a high rail over the wisteria was a grateful cat. She purred and we rode her clear past the watch mongrels behind the iron gate.

Worms on the wet concrete. One yellow daffodil stood erect on a low tide of ground vines. Near the pink house a run of clover reached back to the trash barrels.

Blue clothespins on the wire.

The scent of oranges.

Bright yellow house with an unpainted garage. Black shutters.

The fire berries and bay held the moisture overnight. We turn the leaves and bright water runs down our hands, under our sleeves, over our hard bodies to the road, and on to the storm drains and the underground rivers to the ocean. We are fleas and water, we are stories in the ocean.

Bamboo crowds the roses at a house for sale.

Red pinwheels in the window.

The cats on the way were pleased that we were fleas. The calicos, short hairs, and the cross-bloods with harsh voices and blue eyes paused to hear our stories. They listened and we rode them back to our apartment. Not one wore a flea collar, but there were demons on the block who would fasten collars to the garden statues, houses, power poles, bird feeders, even the birds, and the world.

Soon after we returned from our second tour as fleas at dawn the exterminator parked his truck in the driveway. He ate a few donuts, drank coffee, loaded a tank with chemicals, mounted a new mask and prepared to poison our garden apartment, the last one in the building to be treated with insecticides.

The birds were on the wire and hordes of fleas had enough time to leap out the window and burrow into the seams in his clothes. Other fleas hid in the truck seat and carpets.

Three doves whistled down to the exterminator with the peace fleas cocked on their heads. The doves danced and mourned for peace on the hood of the truck. The exterminator tested the pressure of the tank. He never seemed to notice or hear the doves, much less hear the stories of the mannered peace fleas.

Hawk remembered the fleas on a circus bear who said, "peace on the river and the water dies near the universities." The assault was on and we never had the time to ask him what he meant by that.

The doves bounced on the truck several more times and then flew back to the wire. The peace fleas were so angry over their failure that they leaped to the ground and joined the second assault team, the guerrilla fleas.

"Remember, when the birds turn him back and he takes cover in the truck, then leave the seams and go for the crotch first and suck his blood until he screams," said Market.

The sparrows swarmed and mounted the first avian assault as the exterminator walked toward the apartment with his equipment. The cardinals followed with other birds close behind. The sparrows brushed his head and the other birds shit on his face and shoulders. His mask and gloves were covered with bird shit.

The exterminator waved the enormous rubber gloves at the birds. He moved so fast with anger that he lost one, and when he leaned over to pick up the glove the crows launched their main attack. The crows circled the building and one by one with raucous voices they bounced on his back and pecked at this ears, and pulled his hair. He tried to block the crows and lost his balance, dropped the tank, and ran for cover in his truck.

The crow sorties were precise, and they even continued to pound on the hood of the truck. The other birds dropped their white shit on the windshield. Even the doves shit on the truck once or twice as a gesture of peace.

The fleas were posed for the guerrilla assault on the exterminator. Market lead the first team attack on his crotch. The fleas hit and sucked blood from his crotch more than a hundred times.

Frog lead the second assault team with the dove fleas. They leaped from the seams of his trousers and bit around his asshole. Three fleas burrowed into his ass and the exterminator fainted with pain, and came close to death.

Hawk mounted a message on the dashboard of his truck. The fleas withdrew and when the exterminator was conscious he read the message and never returned to the building. Our garden apartment is a sanctuary once more for birds, bears, fleas, and more in the wanaki game.

Hawk told the exterminator that his blood was poisoned. "The fleas that sucked your blood were chemical mutants, the dead voices of your poison now run in your blood, and the vengeance of the fleas is only the beginning of the war with chemical civilization." The fleas celebrated their liberation from chemicals that night with a dance on the back of a bear.

SQUIRRELS
June 1979

Turn the third card at dawn.

Squirrels in the wanaki circle, squirrels in the north.

The squirrels are with me now on this third turn of the cards. The stones are broken into squirrels and land in the north. We are the squirrels of chance, squirrels turned over on the mountain wind, turned over on the cards. We are squirrels on that slow burn at dawn, down from the treelines to our tribal agonies in the cities.

We are squirrels out on a thin branch, and we run at the dawn with the leaves. The tricksters of the tribe teased us down from the ceremonial birch and pine in the mountains, down from the treelines to new sanctuaries in the wild cities.

Children mount the benches near the lake this morning and train our name with bread and hard peanuts. We bounce and thrash our tails to their lonesome tunes. Once we heard the same trickster stories in the blood and stone as the wordies, but now their prisons in the cities have become our sanctuaries. We rule the trees, the benches near the lake, the boulevards, and the attics in houses that were homesteaded by our ancestors. Domestic pets and wild hawks are taunted by the tricks we do with our tails.

When we turned the corner three blocks from our apartment that morning two bird of paradise flowers opened like the mouths of birds, spread their soft orange beaks and wagged their thin blue tongues. We tricked them with our tails and reached out to touch their bright mouths, to hear their tropical stories. The owner pounded on the window, but we were never shooed by a fist in the distance.

Moist shadows were leashed to their trees.

Fog dogs prowled at dawn in the highest gardens.

The eucalyptus shimmered.

We are squirrels and remembered our stories of the winter demons in the birch and cedar. The ice cracked at night and the crows hounded dead voices on the roads to the reservation. We heard our stories in the stone and took to trees and eaves in the cities.

Sometimes we hide our tails and eat at bird feeders. We chase the wind over the branches, rush the highest trees to see the sun rise over the crowns and coasters, and then lean to the gardens. Far below us the robins listen for worms to move in the moist earth. The sun burns the dead voices, the last words on the outside, and cracks the water beads in the hidden fern. We are squirrels, and our stories run with the water beads out to the stories in the sea.

The juniper reached out from their concrete bunkers. Great boughs of dark green thunder hovered over our shadows at the corner. The blue aromatic berries clear our nose and turn back the bad breath of the cities. Could the juniper berries hold the scent of our stories?

White daisies stand over a bush.

Elusive catbirds whistle deep in the shrubbery. Secrets are remembered.

Twelve columns of bottle brush trees seem to support one side of an old wooden church at the corner of the main street near the lake. The stained glass windows were covered on the inside, a white plastic shade blocked the sacred scenes. Not even the trickster would cover our stories, but that church has a demon in the heart and dead voices at the windows.

We are squirrels on the paw over the cracked concrete in the church parking lot. Seeds gather there, and we hear the weeds would overturn their cover. Our tails brushed the engines under the cars and were blotched with grease.

Nearby, the smell of cedar raised our memories of great trees in the mountains, but we found nothing more than a row of pallid succulents that were surrounded by chemical cedar chips to poison the seeds of wild weeds. We were wild, and would they use poison to hold back our families from the trees? We must go on.

The sun burned the plastic and shattered the scenes in the church windows. We dashed across the busy street in the morning shadows and landed under a band of white birch. What a lucky find in the city. We circled and circled the trees, reached out to the most distant branch and started the summer stories in our blood.

The birch respond to our touch and remember their celebrated clowns from the ancient world, the barren winters near the ocean. The birch were created by the trickster for crows and squirrels and other moral reasons. Even the highest branches were balanced to the touch of our natural bodies. We take giant leaps, rush around the branches, and stage our northern chase scenes to the last leaves. At last we tumble from a fast embrace. The paper bark is smooth, a great sensation so far from home on this third morning in the wanaki game.

The birch told their stories.

The tribal tricksters learned that hunters were wise not to pretend they were better than others on the trail. The spirits hear their stories and a hunter could starve with a cold ear and a mean heart. The tribal hunter could be a dreamer in the birch, and he could become a bear or a bird in his stories. His survival is determined by the stories he remembers at the treeline. Later, the hunter shared his stories with others, and the stories became richer with tricksters, of course, and with each mention.

The wordies, on the other hand, are insecure hunters who compete with each other for their identities and lose their souls to the dead voices. The wordies are wild when they must meditate, and servile when they should be wild to survive the winter with humor. The wordies have lost their stories, and they shoot each other, convinced that hunters are dressed like bear, deer, and moose. The wordies hear too little and see too much. How could a hunter hear a bear in red clothes?

The birch told that a tribal hunter pretended to hear his solace in the birch. He wanted to become the birch in his dreams, and he pretended to be the animal he hunted for food. The tribal hunter walked into the woods alone and searched for a warm place in the sun. He turned his face to the light, rested his back against a tree, and listened to the stories of the birch. He heard crows and squirrels in the distance.

Then the trees and birds and animals were silent. They waited for the hunter to leave. The animals could feel his presence in the woods, and his distance from the natural world. As the tribal hunter rested in the sun he pretended he was part of the birch and the stories of the animals. The hunter became the birch in a word, and he heard the stories of the squirrels, and he wanted his stories to become their stories. His memories moved with ours as squirrels. Could he have become a shaman who hears the birch and our ancient languages?

The hunter pretended to be a squirrel, and we were the hunters.

The hunter had a weapon not a vision.

The hunter raised his small calibre rifle, took aim, and fired at a stout red squirrel as she ran down a birch branch with the wild leaves that autumn. The squirrel snorted once and then tumbled to the ground near the trunk of the tree. The birch wailed, and the birds turned to the blue wind out of the mountains in the west.

Ducks, who ran as smooth as a stone bounced on the water, bounced on the hard leaves, and then there was silence at the death scene. She might have waited out of sight and his stories would be ours tonight.

We were there in our stories with the other squirrels when he aimed and shot. Sudden terror, the shot creased the wind, and then we held to the other side of the birch trunk from the hunter. That one shot was a sound of the great deception of his survival. He would eat once more, and at the same time remain separated from the natural world he tried so hard to remember in his stories. He was wise and waited in the sun, tested our tolerance for boredom, and we lost to his instinct as a hunter. We were too eager to move, to give up our escape distance, and now he has our stories.

Ducks turned over and tried to climb the tree to escape the hunter. The bullet had shattered the bone in her shoulder. Her right front paw was limp, hanging from torn skin and blood soaked hair. The squirrel tried to climb the birch, and each time she reached with the dead paw, she tumbled back into the leaves.

Ducks reached out with the memories of a wild paw, but the paw was not there to hold the birch. She watched the hunter in the distance and tried over and over to climb the tree. Blood ran down her body, down the soft hair on her stomach and spread on her tail. The bright leaves were covered with warm blood. She tried to climb once more and hauled leaves that were stuck to her bloodied hair. Ducks had the stories but not the paws to escape from the hunter.

The hunter watched the squirrel reach to the birch and fired one more shot to end her miseries. The coup de grace was a ruse to end the death throes of a wounded animal and pretend it was an act of compassion. Not a stroke to live, but a shot in the head to end the worries of the hunter.

Ducks would not end her stories. The hunter fired a third time, and then a fourth shot at her head, but she reached out once more and tried to climb the birch. The dead paw laid at her side covered with blood. She reached again and tumbled back into the leaves, and the birch steamed with her blood. That miserable hunter shot her five times.

The first coup de grace tore the fur and flesh

from the top of her head and splattered blood on the paper bark. The bone and thin neck muscles were exposed. Ducks tried to climb the birch with a dead paw and tumbled back into the leaves.

The second coup de grace tore a hole through her cheek and shattered the bones in her lower jaw. Her small teeth were exposed, stained from a rich diet of acorns. Ducks tried to climb the birch with a dead paw and tumbled back into the leaves.

The third coup de grace tore the fur and flesh from her brow and shattered her forehead, but she would not die. She tried to escape from the hunter. Blood bubbled from her tiny nostrils with each breath. Ducks tried to climb the birch with a dead paw and tumbled back into the leaves.

The fourth coup de grace burst one of her eyes and shattered the back of her head leaving a hole that filled with blood and brain. The eyelash twitched over the hole. She had no breath, but she tried one last time to escape from the hunter. Ducks reached out to touch the birch, but she had no paws.

Ducks held the blood soaked leaves and that hunter in one eye. She wanted to be in her own stories, to rush the birch in autumn and hide from the natural demons. The hunter set his weapon to the side and leaned down, closer to the squirrel. His face touched her blood soaked head.

The hunter pleaded to the squirrel, pleaded to be forgiven. He had witnessed a power greater than his own as a hunter, the courage of that squirrel to live had touched his soul. Eye to eye with the squirrel he begged her to forgive him before she died, and he pleaded to her spirit in the birch. The hunter wanted the squirrel to take him into her vision at the end of his stories.

The hunter heard voices in the distance, and then the voices died. He was separated from a world he pretended to understand, and now he was dead in his own stories. Once more the hunter pleaded with the squirrels for forgiveness. The birch was silent. We heard his pleas and held our secrets with the birch.

Ducks blinked once, and then blood bubbled in her nose. Those few bubbles were the last of her breath. The hunter pleaded in tears. Over and over he asked her to forgive what he had done. The blink was her last response, and he heard that as her forgiveness.

The hunter stretched out beside the body of the squirrel. He ran his hand over the hair on her back. The blood was warm. The hunter cried, and his hands were covered with blood. He sang a slow death song without words until it was dark.

Ducks is remembered in our stories. The birch told their stories, and birds sing new songs in the trees near the place where she was shot and died. The hunter wanted to believe that he was forgiven, but his stories were dead voices. The spirit of our squirrel is carried by the birds and becomes the birch.

"The hunter was not forgiven then," said the birch. "He sold his rifle and never thought about hunting again, but he was not forgiven until later when he acted to save a squirrel in the city."

The hunter was driving his car in a residential neighborhood and witnessed a terrible accident. A red squirrel, about the same size as the one he shot, ran across the street near the corner and was hit by a car. The rear tire had crushed his spine and the squirrel could not crawl out of the street. The woman who drove the car was horrified, but she was late for a meeting and asked the hunter to forgive her cruel departure.

The hunter carried the squirrel to the boulevard. He stretched out beside the squirrel, touched his head and paws, and sang a death song. The squirrel never tried to escape. His breath was shallow and he died in peace. The hunter was forgiven at last in the city.

"Could he be a squirrel now?" asked the birch.

"Only in the wanaki game," we said and wondered who would have heard these stories if the birch had not remembered. "Could he be a birch?"

"We have no such game," said the birch.

"Create your own and be remembered in the city."

"You know, squirrels are part birch."

"Then bears are birch," we said and touched the bark.

"Not me, but how can that be?"

"Squirrels are part bear and that makes us birch."

"Yes, we do need our own game," said the birch.

"Wanaki is in the minds that hold the right cards to the city," we said and told her about the pictures and stories of our game. "We could just as well be birch trees."

We were too high in the birch to be worried about the mongrels in the garden, but even so we were the new enemies of domestic pets, our presence touched their lost memories of wild beasts. The trickster was at his best with the mongrels. Could we ever believe that there is wisdom behind the loose tongue on a mongrel?

The primroses wore the very colors that we admired the most in our stories. The blood reds, blues, and yellows were stranded in a new garden that smelled of chemical cedar chips. There was too much space between them in the heat, and so the primroses leaned over to make the most of the morning.

There, on a high porch near the garden a black cat with a blotched white head concentrated on a moth at the screen. The moth moved as the sun reached the porch and the cat leaped a great distance, broke through the mesh, and landed between the red primroses. Naturally, the cat pretended to be interested in the garden and never looked back to the porch. Then she hissed and raised her back at the scent of two squirrels. The moth moved with the sun farther down the screen.

We are squirrels in the garden at dawn and this is our natural game. The twin mongrels at the corner chased after the cat and never noticed that we were squirrels. The mongrels broke through the bamboo fence, pounded over the primroses, chased that cat through the hole in the screen, and beat the hardwood inside the house. We heard the mourning doves on the wire and turned the corner toward the lake.

No one but the fleas bothered us on the bench. They had waited there overnight in the wind checks and wooden cracks for a ride on a human. The fleas were not pleased that we were the first to arrive that morning. We told them stories about the hunters in the birch and the exterminator in the apartment, but we were distracted by a man with a parrot perched on his shoulder. When the man sat down on the bench the fleas were ecstatic and leaped for the blood of an exotic parrot. Sadly, seven fleas were eaten on their best leap so the others decided to avoid the parrot and ride the old man to another bench.

The crows, as usual, were pleased to hear our stories. We pushed past the wire and posed with them in the cage. No one seemed to notice at first, but then the children decided that squirrels should never be locked in cages with mean crows. We pretended without shame to be the squirrels of their rich and serious concern. The peanuts were hard and dead, but one child saved the morning with sunflower seeds. The crows, of course, were raucous that we pretended to be prisoners in this case, but pleased that we had raised the seeds from the same children who abused the crows. Who would believe that crows and squirrels landed in the same birch, and had such a good time at the wanaki games in the city.

# MANTIS
July 1979

Turn the fourth card at dawn.

Praying mantis in the wanaki circle, mantis in the south.

The praying mantis are with me now on this fourth turn of the cards. The stones are broken into praying mantis and land in the south. We are the praying mantis of chance, mantis turned over on the mountain wind, turned over on the cards. We are praying mantis on that slow burn at dawn, down from the wild treelines to our tribal agonies in the cities.

We are praying mantis, the natural inspiration of that famous school of martial arts with the same name, on our last urban adventure from the southern frontier to the ocean cities. We march by ourselves in slow but certain moves, we are trickster twigs on the breeze, our reach is camouflage, wild to the touch.

The bold mantis pennons, earned by the trickster warriors out back in the gardens, and on the high roads to the eucalyptus, were carried by the students who practiced our manner of natural prayer and defense.

Mikado had more pennons than any other mantis, and we carried his colors as praying mantis that morning. He sent us on a reconnaissance mission behind enemy lines in the garden. Our bodies could be black, brown, and green. The green bar on the pennons represented the gardens we had raided, the black our moves, slow and deliberate in the hard brush, and the brown was the silhouette of the way we prayed in our stories.

We were out at dawn in the gardens. Our brown faces and green bodies emerged from the shadows in the wet clover. We were camouflaged and stood on our hind legs with our hands raised in prayer. Our prayers were comic, practical not spiritual, and we were out to catch a meal on the run or wing.

Later the praying mantis planned to move their families closer to the lake, to the rich golden banks of the bay. We waited in the garden and prayed green in dangerous territories that morning. One block south was the public school, and hundreds of children who would be more than eager to capture us in a bottles.

The police services station was located three blocks to the north, and several officers had volunteered to serve the biology teacher at the school, a dubious public relations scheme. She was a practical feminist, unattached, blonde and noticeable, and she wanted praying mantis dead or alive, as many alive as she could find to complete her research on voracious predators. The police never seemed to be surprised that female mantis eat the male at the end of sex.

Mikado was the most disciplined and admired mantis in the gardens, and in the stories of other warrior mantis. His martial moves were practiced by millions of mantis, and his wise dream to create a garden paradise, a wild sanctuary for male mantis, was carried on by his dedicated followers.

"We must endure after sex," said Mikado.

"Indeed, not to be eaten overnight is a basic mantis right," we told the martial mantis. "Even wordies can count on that much in the city, and you deserve more out of sex than sudden death."

"You can say that again," said Mikado.

"The sudden death?"

"Nothing else is hurried."

"Body odor might be the secret weapon."

"Not to me," said Mikado.

"You could make them sick, too sick to eat."

"Road Kill already thought of that," said Mikado.

"Who was that?"

"Never mind, she ate him too."

"You should talk to that biologist who wants our bodies, she studied our sex lives and seems to know more about mantis sex than we do," we said and then remembered that the students and police were not on our side in the matter. "She teaches school and must have a few ideas about how to survive sex."

"Not on your life, not a biologist," said Mikado.

"What could she do?"

"Feed me to the women."

"No, she's a scientist."

"She's a sex demon," said Mikado.

"No, she's a teacher."

"She's a mantis, believe me," said Mikado.

"No, she's a blonde."

"She's a mantis in disguise and she ate my brother."

"You mean she had sex with a mantis?"

"That scientist ate my brother," said Mikado.

"This is more serious than we thought," we said and turned in silence. The notion that a wordy blonde would be aroused by a winged twig was too much to swallow.

"She studied martial arts in my name," said Mikado.

"How could she do that?"

"She prayed to eat my body."

"The first blonde mantis in a public school," we said, but he was much too serious to find any humor in the wordies. "She prays by day, studies our moves, and then eats her research at night."

Mikado prayed in the garden that morning. He was reassured that we would meet with the teacher and talk to her about mantis sexual survival. So, we listened to his stories and learned a few mantis moves to counter what we were told would be the advances of a voracious blonde.

Slowly he climbed as a green twig, and then brown on the wooden fence at the end of the garden. He prayed, and we followed his unusual moves. We were more cautious and held to the lower end of the fence. The fog dogs climbed behind us, and we heard the roar of the ocean in the distance.

Mikado raised his pennon and turned blue in the haze. Closer, his hands were green as he prayed, and then he moved down the high rim on the fence so slowly that only the eagles would notice. The mantis warrior posed with the ghosts. At last the sun burst over the sycamores, and the haze lost once more to the mantis.

Two green flies, fat and out of wind, landed in the sun on the rim of the fence to warm their wings. The martial mantis prayed closer to the wood, as low as a broken twig could bend, and moved to capture the flies. The flies pranced in circles. The secret twig moved closer and closer. We waited on the other end of the fence and tried the same slow moves, so slow that the wind might have moved the mantis.

Mikado held both green flies in his arms, a sudden move and the flies were soon devoured. The morning breeze chased the last ghosts over the fence, the sun warmed our black bodies, and the flies beat their warm wings right down to the end.

The moist remains of the night withered on the rise, over the fence. We were mantis, but our moves were much slower at dawn. "The slower the better to capture flies," the mantis warrior told his students. How slow must a mantis be to survive? Does the sudden end come in slow motion? Would our stories be overheard in the arms of predators?

We had just climbed down from the fence when the celebrated fruit truck parked across the street from the garden. The driver visited a woman once a week and the mantis knew his schedule. The truck was a source of easy food and great humor for the praying mantis.

We never saw so many mantis as we did that morning on the way to the fruit truck. Hundreds of mantis left their best poses in the garden to catch the black flies that sucked the heart of papaya, mango, oranges, lemons, and pears on the back of the fruit truck. The mantis prayed over the fruit and devoured thousands of flies. We wondered if the driver stopped only to shed the flies?

Mikado and his warriors rushed the truck and pretended to sell prayer tickets over the fruit. The mantis hauled the black flies down with their arms and ate so much they could hardly walk back to the garden. Our taste ran closer to the mangoes than the insects. The fruit truck had become a mantis ceremony and so we prayed, closed our eyes, and munched the flies. Actually they were quite plump and juicy, and some tasted like the fruit they had eaten, but otherwise they were rather bland. What turned our stomach was not so much the taste of flies, but what we heard over the fruit. Black flies have their stories, but what we heard that morning was their falsetto death drone. That puny sound of the overwrought flies, the terminal whine and rattle of their wings in the arms of the mantis, was enough to put us off flies forever, and that, to be sure, was the worst part of the ceremony. The rest was an incredible but slow adventure.

Later we were invited to a mantis casino in a eucalyptus grove east of Lake Merritt. We joined the parade and carried our own bright pennon. The sound of so many mantis pennons on the breeze was heard around the world.

This was our first day out as praying mantis and we were part of the fruit truck ceremonies and casino celebrations. The closer we came to the eucalyptus, the more we remembered the fleas, and the more we wondered why the mantis would go there to remember their stories. What was poison to the fleas was an exotic aroma to the praying mantis.

There never seemed to be any answers to the most obvious interests in the world of insects. We heard our creation stories, of course, how the praying mantis were pinched into being by a bear and sent out to eat black flies and other insects that bothered him the most. There, several mantis became warriors and decided to eat the bear. Now that was not a smart move, because the bear taught the female mantis how to eat the male after sex. We heard that was how the problem started.

The praying mantis wear chance on their sleeves, a chance to hear the comic side of their survival. Mantis pray that sex is a chance, and comic survival is on their side. The mantis are slow but not stupid, and everyone knows sex can be a trickster at the right moment, even the wordies. Sex can turn the best minds to comedies, but how do the mantis survive sex with a chance?

The wordies are no better than the mantis. The wordies hear comic in their sex and wear tragic on their sleeves. The mantis are more disciplined and better hunters, and we are wiser with our disguises. The truth must be obvious, the mantis are much smarter than the wordies, because the wordies pretend to be like us and practice praying mantis martial arts. Have you ever seen a mantis pretending to be a wordy at anything?

That night the whole moon tempted the eucalyptus to die in paradise over the casino. We gathered in the bright leaves for the annual celebration, our bear creation and trickster sex from aromatic twigs. The elder mantis warriors prepared seasoned morsels of exotic insects that had been captured in distant gardens, and we drank eucalyptus beer provided by the bear mantis healers. The beer tasted too good to be true.

Mikado has never been without the praise of admirers and the curse of his enemies, even as an adolescent mantis he learned the best disguises to survive in the most dangerous gardens. He was a natural at martial arts, and true as a teacher, but he was bothered most by the bear mantis, the female healers who practiced care politics, and their attention was treacherous to male mantis. We heard many stories that the men who came under the care of the bear mantis were either eaten or became dead voices.

Even so, the warriors were never without mantis women at the casino. They drank too much beer and teased the bear healers. Most of these warriors were eaten overnight. We saw this happen many times, there were the drunken warriors laughing as their bodies were eaten by the bear healers. Once we saw three bears near the end of their meal with only twig legs stuck out of their mouths.

Mikado told his warriors that the future has no future tense, but he reminded them that he was not prepared to be eaten in the past tense either. He was blinded by sex but somehow he survived the care of the bear healers. The stories we heard were true, he was the wise mantis, the one who courted the demons and survived in various disguises that confused even the most devious healers.

That night at the casino celebration he invited more mantis women than we could count to soak their twigs in the stream. He soaked his whole body in eucalyptus water three times a year as protection. Naturally, there was more to the soak than met the ear. The bear mantis hated him, but the other women adored him, some even wove new pennons in praise of his vision as a wise mantis warrior. We heard that mantis care and adoration was a disguise, but his chance to survive had become a legend, and a tasty temptation at the same time. One bear mantis told us the warrior was a masturbator, but most mantis women were convinced that he was the first mantis who prayed coitus interruptus, a new martial art that he learned from the wordies.

Mikado boasted that he had soaked his twigs beside hundreds of bear mantis without so much as a bite mark to his name. Such stories tempted the bear mantis and radical healers to lure him to his proper end. In fact, that night we were surprised to hear so many healers at the hard feet of the warrior in the stream. Their care, we learned later, was a cruel deception to capture and devour him with or without sex.

Mikado seemed unaware or unconcerned that he was about to become the sacrificial victim of the bear healers at his own casino celebration in the eucalyptus. He said it was the best expression of civilization that he could imagine, to act like a word and end like a mantis.

"The wordies are like the praying mantis, we were made out of twigs by the bear, and they were made out of dirt by a spirit, but now they make a mountain out of words," said Mikado.

The healers were very excited because the hour was near when each of them would feast on a part of his hard body. No such thing happened because we warned him that he was about to be devoured, but something even more incredible took place that night. As you might have expected we were scorned by the bear mantis.

The blonde learned from her spies that the praying mantis were at the eucalyptus casino that night. So, she organized her students and the police volunteers, armed them with bottles, lids, and flashlights, and commanded a ruthless assault on our celebration. We were created to pray slower than the wordies, and because of our natural pose, thousands of mantis were captured in bottles that night for indentured research. Only a few prayed undercover in the brush and escaped the cruelties of the wordies.

Mikado was in a container next to ours when we were first captured. He stood high in the glass and prayed on his own reflection. He was in the mantis center of our survival stories in the city. We praised his wisdom and practices as a mantis warrior. Later, in the school laboratory, we shared the same glass cage that had been furnished to look like a miniature eucalyptus casino. Nearby, the bear warriors sneered and mocked our moves. How many generations does it take to lose the stories of creation and the mission to devour male mantis?

The blonde visited the glass cages at night and the students studied our sex habits by day. The blonde might have asked the mantis what she wanted to know, or she could have played the wanaki game, but that would have ended her scientific power. We would exist the way she discovered and studied praying mantis. We were no longer the mantis of our stories in the city, we were laboratory mantis. Our stories would die at the end of their studies, and we would end in the dead voices of the wordies.

Mikado was astounded when we told him about the wanaki game, and that our presence as praying mantis was a chance turn of the cards. He said such games were mantis stories, that mantis created the cards. The mantis seem to be responsible for so many things.

"The trickster created the stones, and the stones became bears, and the bears created the praying mantis, and in that way the mantis created the cards," we said and leaned back on the eucalyptus leaves in the cage.

"That blonde might listen to you," said Mikado.

"Not as praying mantis."

"She's worse than sex, the laboratory is our end."

"Some blondes are mantis healers."

"Wordies are never that smart," said Mikado.

"So, how do we get out of here?"

"The bear healers must know a way out."

"We must turn a new wanaki card."

"Turn the seasons, turn a bear," said Mikado.

"The blonde would never hear our stories."

"Have you ever been more than a mantis?"

"Yes, we were fleas last month."

"Then you are a warrior survivor," said Mikado.

"We turn the cards."

"Mantis have the power of camouflage, we stand as twigs, and we can turn brown on the fence and green in the garden," said Mikado. He raised his hands and paced to the end of the cage as he lectured. "Mantis pose and change colors, but we never had the chance to be some other creature, so we have no way to bring that power out of our bodies as we can our pose and colors."

"Too bad you missed the chance at the cards."

"You have been a flea, and you have that secret in your mantis body now," he raised his voice and paced to the other end of the cage. "You must meditate, you must hear how to be that flea in your memories, that flea is in your blood forever."

Mikado was right, our stories of the fleas never ended with the turn of the cards. We were bears, squirrels, fleas, and more. He told us meditation stories and soon our mantis body seemed to rise and move in the cage. We could still hear his voice, but he was at a great distance.

At last we were fleas again, and when the

blonde opened the cage to feed ants and other insects to the mantis, we leaped out and rode her hair to the classroom that morning. Later, when the coast was clear, we leaped out the window and rode a mongrel back to the apartment.

Tiny flies were stalked in the dragon lilies, and the sparrows were very angry that morning. Wild roses reached out from a vacant lot to be remembered by the fleas and the praying mantis. Someone staked a blue heart and a scarecross in the garden.

The weed forests behind our building were ruled by new colonies of red ants from the mountains. They marched into the center, climbed out on the highest leaves, and then bent the weeds down to the ground. They climbed and felled weeds forever, and their children marched to other forests and downed weeds, a natural right of the ants. They work so hard for such a common pleasure, and they have a nasty sting. We wondered if they might be interested in bringing down a blonde?

The floor of our apartment was decorated with twigs and praying mantis parts, and the stones were spread in a wide circle. Once more we turned the mirrors and remembered the stories of the bear, the stories in the blood. The bears were there at dusk. We were bears in the mirror.

We were bears and we waited for the blonde to land alone in her laboratory later that night. She carried dinner and pushed the door open with her buns, out of breath and balance. We rushed her from the side, roared and beat on the door, but she pretended not to hear. She was so rational that if we were not wordies, or could not be seen in printed words, then we were not there at the end of the word. We pushed more and tore the buttons on her blouse. She hesitated but did not show any sign of fear until we ate her hamburger and roared her name over and over in the laboratory. She screamed at last and ran from the room when we wrote the word blonde and our name on the chalkboard.

Mikado was amused, but we were reminded that the mission was to liberate the praying mantis, even the bear healers, and then pound fear into the heart of that cold blonde. We raised the metal covers and carried the glass cages out in the field behind the school building. Overnight the mantis walked back to their gardens and told stories about science in the city.

Mikado was the last to leave the laboratory that night. He rode on our shoulder back to the apartment. He admired the mirrors, the wanaki circle, and demanded that we both turn cards in the game. We insisted that he turn the first card, and he turned the picture of the trickster. He touched the picture, never hesitated to decide that the trickster would be a blonde to catch another blonde in school.

# CROWS
September 1979

Turn the fifth card over at dawn.

Crows in the wanaki circle, crows in the south.

The crows are with me now on this fifth turn of the cards. The stones are broken into crows and land in the south. We are the crows of chance, crows turned over on the mountain wind, turned over on the cards. We are crows on that slow burn at dawn, down from the wild treelines to our tribal agonies in the cities.

We are crows, brisk and alive to the wild glance, and we survived the dead voices of the corn farmers over the barrel of a shotgun. We heard the best glances in the poplar and birch, and held the last glance of a woman on a snowmobile. She lost her head over the crows on a wire fence.

Crows hear their enemies and see the word-ies. Crows caw to those who envy wings, and those who would rather be black. We live on the brisk glance as natural as a sudden summer in the spring, or circus snakes in a bear cage.

The choice glances of children at the window and lonesome prisoners at the wire are never undone in dead voices. That wide stream of dust behind a school bus was an abandoned glance. Scarecrows, blue hearts at the corner, masks out of trickster time, and bursts of pure radiance that once stained our sacred shrouds, are the glances that crows remembered in their stories.

More than that, we are the trickster crows behind the sudden laughter of the wordies, we are the crows in their dreams, we are the crows who tried to save them from their dead voices.

The crows and dust streams run with the wind, but the children on the buses are buried at the source in the dead voices of education. The glances run out, word by word in chalk and glazed talk in laboratories, and the pale wordies lose the touch of crows and their stories in the blood.

There were crows behind the wordies, crows that once healed with blue wings and trickster stories. We heard the crows heal the wounded and caged birds in the cities. At dusk the crows raised the windows with their caws. The wild birds turned in magical flight. The wordies were held back by their dead voices.

We were perched in the sycamores and cawed our stories out to the prisoners at dawn. The glance of moist air brightened the gardens and the metal in the city. Below, the roof of a playhouse, laid out in the backyard of a child care center, was painted orange and blue, the shape of a bird in flight. The red wagons were parked in a row near the swings.

We circled and cawed as the children arrived at the center, and later we pounded on the orange roof until the children heard the commotion and came out to play. Rain or shine, but never on time, the children feed us stale crackers from the wagons out back. We were pleased, but you can be sure there was more to our performance than a few crackers.

Moses, the senior crow in sight of the sycamores, posed on the edge of the playhouse, thrust his beak at the bright slivers of sunlight, strutted and crow danced on the metal to hold the casual glances of the children. We wondered where he found his food, because he never ate child care crackers with us out of the wagons.

That old crow shamed us to dance for the crackers, and so we thrust and parried with our beaks, hopped, stretched and flapped in circles, stared from side to side, and cawed at the end to scare the children.

There must be a better connection to the

sacred stones and natural memories in the crow world than sour children at school in the morning. Child care on the concrete bruised their stories and healed ours, the stories children might have told on their own in the weeds behind the garage. They needed a trickster crow in their hearts to survive the dead voices in the city. So, we taught them how to caw and crow dance on the corner.

Moses was the best crow dancer on metal and concrete, a trickster on the hard roads of the wordies. He ducked his head and coasted, crouched and turned, like no other bird or beast, and he did it better than any crow in the city. He came from a long line of wise dancers in the birch. Even the stones turned to hear when he cawed and bounced out his stories for the children. How could there ever be a better show of our creation than a crow dance?

Some children were bored and never raised their heads to hear the birds, or even the seasons. Others were cruel and tried to capture us with nets tied to long sticks, but the older crows hardly noticed. Some children hated the idea that crows were black and could dance and fly out of their reach, so they threw stones and tried to jerk our tail feathers out. How were they to know that we were tricksters in the stones?

Moses said the dance was more important than our worries over tail feathers, "because the children do the same cruel things to cats, dragonflies, and each other, and who knows what would become of cats and crows if we were never hated by someone."

"The trickster stone was hated at creation."

"Stones break, crows dance too much for the wordies."

"Their voices died so soon."

"Children may never hear their stories," said Moses.

"That bored child under the swings might glance at the crows and notice our black bodies posed at creation," we said. "How would a cruel child ever hear that we were stones, and crows, and bears?"

Moses mounted a windmill on a pole over the swings and bounced on the paddles that drove the mill. Two metal figures, fastened to a cam, sawed a piece of wood faster and faster on the wind, and the children of the wordies shouted at the old black wind and danced around the pole.

The lemons were brushed with a scent of mould.

Plastic crucifixion in the window.

Three dead birch pruned in half a barrel.

We were crows on the rise that morning and we could wait no longer for innocence, so we cawed out the lions to scare the children. Small lions that purred at first, and then lions that roared, and at last lions that pounded their huge paws in circles on the concrete. The children were steadfast for the first time in their lives, even the screamers were silent.

"Look, the lions want a ride," said a

screamer. He pointed to the red wagons, but no one heard him because his voice was a whisper compared to his usual screams.

The lions even raised a few glances for the crows. "Look at the black birds sawing wood," said the bored children who heard us on the windmill. We stretched our wings, ducked, and cawed to the end of boredom at the child care center.

Moses soared down, landed on the lion, and crow danced from his tail to his head. The lion purred and the children churred. Encouraged by the natural sounds, we bounced on their heads, mussed their hair, and at last the children started to dance on the concrete. There were crows, cats, lions, and various domestic creatures, hand-to-mouth at the child care center.

The teachers were amused at first, the children pretended to be the very beasts and birds they once tormented, but then the sounds were more natural, the dances wild, and the children cawed as crows, roared as lions, and pounced on the teachers. One teacher was wounded on the heels by two lions, the crows bounced on a blonde and turned her over, and an older teacher ran in terror as a beast tried to bite her head. The children heard the stories in their blood and that morning one child care center turned wild in the city.

"Teach me how to fly," shouted a wild child crow.

"Dream the wind," said Moses.

"No, that's not the way," said the child.

"Maybe you're not a crow."

"No, teach me to be a lion then," said the child.

"Crows never turn to lions," said Moses.

"No, that's not true," said the child.

"Crows are wiser, crows teach the lions to roar," said Moses.

"Lions pound the concrete, crows are tricksters, crows dream," we told the children. "So, if you want to fly you have to dream the wind and imagine flight, that's how we did it, and you can fly from here right to the windmill, just like a crow with stories."

"Would my arms grow wings?"

"Dream crow and your feathers turn black," said Moses.

"How about blue?" asked the child.

"Dream crow and blue wings," said Moses.

"I could just wear some wings and then take them off to ride my bicycle," said the child. He pushed the crows in a red wagon from one end of the concrete to the other.

"Does your bicycle have training wheels?"

"No, it does not," shouted the child.

"How come you would dream a color before you had wings?" we asked the child. He had taken a glance at the crows, pretended to be wild in a crow dance, and then he turned to feathers and colors and the avoidance of the wordies.

"Can crows have red feet?"

"Why would you want so many colors?"

"Black is boring," said the child.

"You could end up with a closet full of bird parts in different colors, like so many socks or shirts," we told the child. "You might have the best colors and the right parts, but no stories that raise you to the trees."

The teachers returned and ordered the child crows and lions back into their cages in the child care center. They cawed and roared back at the nervous teachers.

"Something got into them this morning," said a teacher.

"Sugar, too much junk food," said the blonde.

"Put the wagons back where they belong," shouted the only male teacher at the center. Three children parked the wagons, traced the cracks in the concrete with the toes of their shoes, hesitated on the stairs, and then raised their arms and pretended to fly one last time. They so wanted to escape from their education that morning. Later, the children waved to the crows from the window.

Moses amused the children with a wounded crow dance. He bounced on the stones, spread his great wings, and turned blue right there outside the window. The children pressed their tongues to the glass and have never been the same since then. The stories of their wild time that morning ended with a glance from a cage.

Moses circled the center a few times and then flew high above the city, out of human sight, far from the wordies and their dead voices. We were crows and our stories were heard in the blood, in the distance. Who would remember that we were tricksters in the stone?

Lake Merritt shimmered in the bright light far below. We soared in wide circles and landed on the crow cage in the park. The eagle watched from the cage across the path. We crow danced on the wire and the wounded crow inside moved from side to side on the perch, but he could have been in a child care center. We dreamed his breaks in the wire, but the crow refused to leave the cage.

Moses shouted to the crow, "why would you be a prisoner?"

The caged crow turned on the perch. He avoided our glances and was silent at first, but then he said, "my wounds are an advantage, the cage is my solace, my protection from the wild outside."

"Cages are no protection," said Moses.

"They are when the door is open," said the caged crow.

"Protection is a condition, not a cage."

"Once a day, without fail, the park attendant leaves the door open for a few hours," said the caged crow. "I broke a wing and was poisoned by the city, and since then got tired of flying to survive my next meal on the road."

"Crows are the condition," said Moses.

"When the cage is open no one leaves, no one enters."

"No one listens, prison is a dead voice," said Moses.

"Granted there are days when the children disguised stones as chunks of their lunch, but nothing is worse than hanging out at a school," said the caged crow. "I went to them once, now they come to me, and in any case the park attendant is sure to feed me on time every day."

Moses was worried that a crow had weakened his stories in the cage, so he called in the tricksters and trained several possum to eat crow food as soon as the park attendant left the cage. Naturally, the crow cawed for more, but he went hungry for days. The attendant was fed up with the crow and his constant noise, so he decided the crow was healed enough to be on his own once more. The attendant shooed the crow out and locked the cage, and the crow cawed for mercy. The trickster possum lost interest in the lesson and moved to other cages. The crow learned to eat outside, but he never lost sight of the cage.

"The wordies touched that crow," said Moses.

"Turn him into a possum."

"Good idea, the possum that would caw."

"How about a flea?" we asked.

"The flea that cawed is a better prison," said Moses.

"So, what's the dance for that?"

"Turn the wanaki cards, you figure it out."

"The fleas won't like this," we said.

"They care about blood not feathers," said Moses.

"Here he goes from crow to flea," we said and turned the picture of the flea on the wanaki cards. We were there and remembered the stories, the wild rides in hair and feathers. Maybe the crow would like the determined search for blood.

Moses pretended we needed to turn the flea card, but actually he could have imagined the crow as just about anything. Fleas were nothing to create. Remember, he turned his wings blue and lions loose at the child care center, and never thought much about it either.

"Why do you punish me?" asked the caged crow.

"You punish our stories as crows," said Moses.

"Why is it so wrong to be a tired crow, to depend on a good cage and regular meals?" asked the crow who was a flea. The crow was so angry that he had been forced from his comfortable cage and turned into a flea that he did everything he could to make life miserable for the crows.

Moses could not believe that he was so dedicated to get even with the crows, those who conspired to make him a common flea. "He must have given as much energy to live in that cage as he does to hating crows."

"Fleas hang on, you can be sure of that, but

disease is the only real threat, and they move on." We worried that we had wronged the crows over a cage, and betrayed the stories of the fleas.

Moses complained that the crow flea rode on his wings and tried to suck him down in flight. "He sucked blood from under my wing and we almost crashed into a window."

"Turn him back to stone over the lake."

"I tried, but he won't change when he's sucking my blood," said Moses. "I imagined he was everything from a snake to a duck, but he knows my blood is his protection, and he's determined to suck me dry."

"We know exactly how to shed fleas," we boasted.

"Get with it then," said Moses.

"Follow us," we said and flew to the secret eucalyptus casino near the lake. We remembered the stories from our time as praying mantis. Moses soaked his feet in the eucalyptus stream, splashed his wings on the aromatic water, and then thrashed his head and body in the stream. The crow flea hung on with spite far longer than any other flea would have endured, and then leaped to the shore.

Moses carried such powerful thoughts about turning the crow flea into a bear, that as soon as the crow had leaped to shore he became a bear before his feet hit the ground. The bear growled and roared and chased the crows in the eucalyptus. We teased him to be sure it was the crow flea, and then flew out of his sight.

The crow bear traveled with a circus, lived in a cage, rode a bicycle in a circle, wore a blue scarf, bowed to the applause of wordies and their children, and was fed very well for what he did seven nights a week. The cage was private, and the cage protected him from the outside. The last stories we heard were from the circus, the crow bear was happier as a bear than he had ever been as a crow. For one thing, children respected him and no one threw stones into his cage at the circus. He was big enough to have his own flea families, he rode a bicycle, and he told the local crows that he would rather be a bear than a crow, because bears are feared and would never be turned from their cages.

The crow stories ended in our apartment. Two black feathers held one side of the wanaki circle, and the crows laughed in the stones from one corner to the other. Moses gave me one of his feathers and we placed it in the north, our stone memories. At dusk we had very little to return to the natural world in the city. No flowers or leaves, only feathers and stones in the circle. We turned inward for the night as crows do in their stories.

BEAVER
October 1979

Turn the sixth card over at dawn.

Beaver in the wanaki circle, beaver in the north.

The beaver are with me now on this sixth turn of the cards. The stones are broken into beaver and land in the north. We are the beaver of chance, beaver turned over on the mountain wind, turned over on the cards. We are beaver on that slow burn at dawn, down from the wild treelines to our tribal agonies in the cities.

We are beaver on the run this morning, beaver from under the dawn. We are the river beaver, and our broad tails were once delicacies to the tribes. Then the wordies discovered our rivers and stole our stories and left us with their dead voices.

The gentlemen of the time wore felt hats pounded from our best hair. We were saved by the turn of fashions, a chance survival, but not before we were brought close to our woodland end by the fur traders. Now we find solace in the wild cities. The new fur traders are more obvious here, and our survival comes with stories not water.

The whole moon was brighter in the west just before dawn. We were out on the moist streets close to the treelines, a natural habit of beaver in the city. The snails moved deep in the wet grass. Flies circled in the first glances of sunlight to warm their wings.

Near that house with the blue heart a woman towed a miniature beast on a leash. We tried to hide but the curly beast rushed over the boulevard and pushed his wet nose in our crotch. His breath was rude and smelled of bad meat.

The woman was a nervous wordy and wagged her pure hands as she laughed, a practiced melody on the rise, and she pranced in the wet grass, but did nothing to haul her beast out of our crotch. We were certain the perfume she wore so early in the morning came from our stories, and it was probably castor, that familiar wild scent that confused the domestic beast. We took pity on him in the end, he could hardly smell the difference between a beaver and a nervous wordy. She must have been searching for a beaver. Why would she wear our scent so early in the morning?

"Fuss is confused over something," said the woman.

"Must be something, the early morning is so wild," we said. Fuss must wonder what his nose is telling him outside, are people animals or not, birds, bears, or maybe beavers? Fuss snorted with pleasure in our crotch.

Finally we smacked our tail on the grass and scared the beast. Fuss ran behind his wordy and pranced on her shoes. She said he could bark out the time, he was very smart.

"We knew a dog who called wingo at bingo games."

"Forgive me, but who is we?"

"We are beaver in the wanaki circle."

"Forgive me, but we are late," said the woman. She backed out of our conversation, turned on the sidewalk, and crossed the street in a hurry. The wordy and her beast were both very nervous. The beast started to shiver so she carried him the rest of the way home.

We were the beaver of fresh water who turned from the scented traps and landed in the cities to escape the fur traders. We were the water tricksters and dam builders, and we heard stories in the touchwood and luminous bearwalks that were natural at night on the great river in the woodland.

We were beaver and tasted the tender trees

in the gardens on the block, a clean bite, not enough to leave an obvious wound. The live oak were on one side of the lake, hard and bitter, the incense cedar were smooth and mellow on the other side, and the palm were baked, dried, and tasteless. The bay laurel were pungent, the warm bottle brush tasted sour, and the mock orange had no taste that would ever be remembered. Nothing on the block could compare to the sweet aspen and birch trees near the great river.

The houses were brushed with dew, the stones carried leaves until morning, and the inside plants pressed on the windows to be outside in the autumn. The leaves carried their stories in an aura, and where the leaves have been there is a bright trace in the tree. The trace of an aura holds the natural shape of cut and broken leaves. How do beaver leave their traces in the water?

That big ginger cat sat beside the fern. He yawned and turned his whiskers on the breeze outside the basement window of a house near the middle of the block. The ginger had six toes on both front paws. The toes were his traces on the stone. The early sunlight cornered the dew on the low windows. The ginger watched the other cats as they posed on the rim and roamed on the block.

Several inside cats lurked beside the plants in windows, and others spied under porches and cars at the curb. Two cats howled on the fence in the garden at the corner. Some of the cats followed at a distance, they must have smelled our castor. Their gaze was wild, and the hair on their noses moved to remember the stories of the scent. We were beaver in the city and the cats heard the wild but could not remember the trace of our castor in their stories.

"Terrocious, this is absolutely terrocious," said the shrouded woman over and over. She turned over the cover on a storm sewer and shouted down into the dark manhole. "Come out, come out you nasty demons, come out into the bright light."

"Terrocious, what ever could be terrocious?"

"Terrocious, of course, a new word coined by combining terrible and ferocious," said the woman. She was older than the sewer, muscular, and her head was covered, but her hair must have been wild and white. She seemed to glow, but when we tried to see her face she moved her head down, or turned to the side.

"Do you live here?" we asked the woman.

"Not on your life," she shouted.

"Those covers are very heavy."

"Not really," she said, and shouted into the hole.

"Why are you shouting down there?"

"Don't be stupid," she shouted.

"Then tell us who's down there," we insisted and leaned over the manhole. Her voice echoed in the sewer, and we heard water and distant thunder. The cats were curious and one by one they came to the edge of the manhole. There, the big ginger laid his many toes on the rim and looked into the sewer. The other cats leaned closer to the edge. They listened and sniffed the foul breath from the dark and dangerous manhole.

The thunder could have been a summer storm, but the sound came from cars pounding over other sewers in the distance. We waited with the cats for something to happen, a withered hand reaching out from the sewer, a sinister voice, or at least an explanation from the woman who raised the grate and shouted to the demons in the manhole. Nothing happened, and when we turned the woman had vanished.

We heard her laugh and saw her turn the corner on the run. By the time we caught up to her she was close to the lake. The big ginger followed us but the other cats would not leave the sewer until something happened in the manhole. The sewer was covered later, but the cats continued to visit the site, the trace of the unknown. Some cats peered into the small holes on the cover, and others pushed their paws down the holes. Nothing ever happened, but the cats took that sewer into their stories of the city.

The old woman picked things up on the path, feathers, leaves, and other bits of nature, as she walked around the lake. She was mocking our game, but we missed the play at first because we were so curious and hurried on her trail. At last she landed outside the empty crow cage near the lake and we had a chance to ask her once more about the sewer.

"You tricked us over the sewer," we told the old woman.

"Nobody ever tricks anyone."

"You shouted into that sewer and left us there."

"Nobody left you there," she said and turned her head.

"What was in the sewer?"

"Thunder, the water demons, who knows?"

"But why did you open that particular man-hole and leave us there, and why so early in the morning?" we asked and tried to see her face. She wore a print dress, and a scarf covered her head and most of her shoulders. She carried a plain cloth purse, and when we moved closer she swung the purse to the side and drew the scarf over her face. The old ginger purred between our legs.

"Would you like to see my face?"

"Of course we would."

"Why me in the morning?" asked the old woman.

"Because, you seem so familiar."

"You see, my face could be a mirror."

"Easier to remember then."

"You wonder, could she be a trickster?"

"Who else would shout into a sewer at dawn?"

"Tricksters are stories not real people."

"We know those stories," we told the old woman.

"The trickster is a hand in masturbation, you can bet on that, the hand and stories are real, but nobody is there," said the old woman. She opened the cage, the same one the crow held until we rousted him, climbed inside and leaned on the wire. The old ginger followed her into the cage. "You heard the trickster and came to the sewer with your cats, but the trickster was you, not me."

"You are the trickster, we are beaver."

"Would you be a stone?"

"We are stones in our stories," we told the old woman.

"Come closer to the cage, come closer to me, remember me in your stories, remember you heard she was the old woman who was never there," she said and then turned to face us at the wire.

The old woman raised the scarf and died in a ball of light. She had a luminous head and the loose shape of a face. The light was bright, but there were no bones or real flesh on the face. The luminous head moved with colors as muscles would, and her eyes were dark and dangerous in the ball of light. She had covered the luminous stories of a trickster. The big ginger hissed at the light and ran back home.

"Naanabozho is my name," said the old woman.

"You have the same name as the trickster who created the earth, but how can you be here in a crow cage?" The crows cawed in the distance, and we might have told the stories about the crow who turned out to be a circus bear.

"Tricksters are stories, there are no tricksters but a hand in the night," she said and untied the ties at her waist, "Even so, you must remember me as a trickster, because who else can do things with shit that make people laugh so much?"

"Naanabozho made wordies out of shit."

"The trickster made the very first anthropologists out of shit," said the old woman. She raised her dress, squatted near the perch, and shit right then and there in the crow cage. "Now, let's see how many anthropologists we can make out of shit this morning."

Naanabozho had to be a wild figure in a trickster story or else no one would ever believe what she could do with shit. Trickster stories have been told since the stones and tribes were created, and we all know that the trickster made anthropologists out of shit, but who would believe that a real woman dumped in a crow cage and created a new school of anthropologists near Lake Merritt.

"Anthropologists end up in the sewers," said Naanabozho. She wiped her hands and tied the waist on her dress. Crows heard the shit stories and circled overhead. "What a waste, the crows and anthropologists never did learned how to shape and shift their own shit."

"So, is that why you raised the cover this morning?"

"No, there was nothing there, the sewer was a chance to catch cats and beaver over nothing," said the trickster. "My, my, and we caught the beaver of the day over a trickster sewer." She laughed and the wild sound burst from her luminous head. The crow cage was lighted, and thousands of cold insects rushed to the heat. Black flies circled her head in wide bands but no one ever touched the trickster. The heat was real to the crows and insects, but not the trickster.

"How did you know we would be there?"

"How could the beaver resist trickster creation stories over a sewer in the city?" asked Naanabozho. She had a new version of creation that turned the great flood into a sewer of anthropologists.

When the very first trickster was up to his nose in the great flood he asked some animals to dive down and come back with a few bits of sand so she could start a new world. The beaver and others dove down and one of them came back with enough for the trickster to make a new world.

Naanabozho told the the new stories of creation in the city. "The last time we had to dive through shit shaped anthropologists to find the remains of the tribal world and create a new one," said the trickster. She smiled and there was a trace of blue light on her hands.

"So, we should dive into the sewer?"

"No, but a terrocious accident happened right there in that sewer," she said and leaned over a pond in the crow cage. There was no reflection, the water would not hold her luminous head.

"Get to the terrocious parts," we insisted.

"This is a creation story about a crossblood blonde with webbed toes who could swim faster than anyone in the world. She might have saved the tribe in the great flood. She was a cheerleader, and on her way to school one morning she heard that seductive purr and distant thunder deep down in the sewer and vanished in the manhole," said the trickster who had created her out of shit to tease the teachers. "Now, the school shaman heard that domestic cats were the only animals who could rescue the blonde, but her teachers were not certain that the cats would cut the shit to save a blonde.

"They were right, the cats, black, white, and calico, refused to wade into the shit in the sewer, so the trickster created an anthropologist out of shit, named him Shicer, a doctor in the new school of tribal care and rescue, and sent him deep down into the sewer to find the cheerleader."

"So, did he find her in the shit?"

"Shicer was very proud to be the first rescue anthropologist made out of shit, and the first to be asked to dive into the underworld of demon shit to save the crossblood cheerleader, the pride of the tribe in the city.

"Shicer landed at the bottom of the sewer and heard that distant thunder, the wild drums over the manhole covers, but he could not see the end of the tunnel so he touched his way in the thick water and whistled a happy tune from the new school," said the luminous trickster.

"Naanabozho asked the beaver to do the same thing at the creation after the great flood," we told the trickster. "The trickster was up to his nose in water, and his own turds floated close to his nose, so he asked the beaver to dive down and rescue the last of the old earth, but it was the muskrat who came back with a little bit of sand, enough for the tribe to pack a new island on the back of a turtle."

"Shicer had no such luck," said Naana-bozho. "The blonde he found in the sewer held him so close that their bodies melted one into the other, and no one could figure out how to pull that shit apart."

"So, how did they get out?" we asked the trickster.

"What seems to be a game is not a game, the opposites are never the other, the plurals, even the pronouns we write, are not in the natural world, and one plus one comes to shit in a blonde and anthropologist, so we pushed the curious domestic cats into the sewer to separate the shit, and somehow that ginger cat with the six toes came back with parts of the pair," said Naana-bozho.

"You mean the big ginger ate shit?"

"She shouted 'raise the cover and lend me a paw' and then climbed out backward with a double hand and two ears of shit in her mouth, and later she hauled out their melted heads, " said the luminous trickster. "The other cats purred over the remains in the sewer, but the big ginger was the only cat that came back."

"What happened to their heads?" we asked the trickster.

"The blonde and the anthropologist became a mutant in their heat, a sewer creature on the city," said Naanabozho. "The big ginger sat there at the rim of the manhole and watched the cross-blood head turn into a rescue anthropologist, and then their heads melted with the last of the webbed toes in the tribe, back into the sewer."

"So, are they the purr we heard this morning?"

"The tribal mutants purred and teased the demons in the sewers, and their sound became much louder and heated the corner," said the luminous trickster. "The big ginger knew the secret, and there were stories about the underworld of lost cats, but no one could figure out what caused the purr, or the light at the end of the sewer.

"Everybody knows that shit gives off a gas, and even more in this case, but no one expected that blonde and anthropologist to turn green and shoot a light out of the holes in the sewer cover," said the trickster. "That big purr and then the weird light at night started some incredible stories.

"The man who lives across the street from

the manhole said he saw two white cowboy boots and a pink pony come out of the sewer and dance, and then a man around the corner told everybody that he saw a giant calico cat that glowed in the dark and ate dogs," said the trickster. "Other people told stories about giant cats, great balls of light, and thin demons in streams on the street down to the lake, but no one was too worried until people started to lose their hair and vision."

"The wordies were going bald and blind?"

"Yes, and people were scared so they called in the federal government to see what sort of tribal evil had been poured into the sewers that would cause wordies to lose their sight."

"How about getting old?" we asked the trickster.

"They were so taken with the purr and the light in the sewer that the wordies forgot their own stories about getting old," said Naana-bozho. "They never had many stories to start with, so they were distracted by weird lights and purrs from the underground until they needed glasses."

"So, what did the government do?"

"They sent out two anthropologists who were experts on witchcraft to see what was the matter with the sewer," said the luminous trickster. "The two were fearless scientists, naturally, and so they climbed down into the sewer and never returned.

"Now, you might think, as many people do,

that they were taken with the same blonde as the first anthropologist, but it turned out to be a bit more complicated because the two never knew they were fashioned out of shit until they were part of the underground, and once there, faced with their ultimate trickster origins, they embraced their own shit in the sewer."

Naanabozho was no more than a trace of light when we turned back to the crow cage. She had vanished at the end of the stories on sewer rescues and the crossblood blonde. She left behind her cloth purse, and when we leaned over to pick it up a crow bounced on our head and landed on the perch in the cage. Could it be that the crow we had turned into a flea and then a circus bear was back in his cage?

Later, we heard in stories told by a black panther that the bear, who was once a cage crow, beat his circus trainer with a bicycle, bit two children, ate three dancing dogs, and then became a trickster with a luminous head. She came back to the lake to haunt his enemies, the wordies, the beaver, and the old crow in the city. He ruled the sewers with shit demons and then retired once more as a crow in a cage.

Nothing has ever been the same since the trickster turned the blonde and the anthropologist into melted shit and dead voices in the city. Black flies and other insects have been sucked into the holes on the sewer cover.

Lake Merritt held the bright trees on the surface, and leaves floated over the broken water treelines. We rushed to the flea bench near the end of the lake and opened the cloth purse. Inside, there were buttons, twigs, feathers, seeds, two coins, and many stones taken from the path around the lake. The luminous trickster might have taken over our game if she had not tired and returned to his perch as a crow.

We were river beaver on the run back to our apartment. We circled the sewers on the block to avoid the odor of the anthropologists. Their shit could wound tribal children at night, and their demonic light could ruin our stories in the city.

The cats were in their windows, and the big ginger purred beside the tender fern. We turned the mirrors to hear the bears in our stories. In the distant light we placed one stone in the circle for each cat on the block, and the stones from the cloth purse became the wordies who turned to shit. The floor of our apartment was covered with stones. We are stones broken in the wanaki game.

Once we carved our beaver sticks from the sweetest aspen and birch to build our houses on the great river, and then we poked the shit demons back into the sewer, and set our sticks to purr in the wanaki circle. One card waited to be turned. We were beaver near the end in the city.

TRICKSTERS
December 1979

Turn the last card over at dawn.

Tricksters in the center of the wanaki circle.

The tricksters are with me now on this seventh turn of the cards. The stones are broken into tricksters and land in the four directions. We are the tricksters of chance, tricksters turned over on the mountain wind, turned over on the cards. We are tricksters on that slow burn at dawn, down from the wild treelines to our tribal agonies in the cities.

The trickster turned his back on the ocean and watched the rain beat the gardens near the corner. The ferns were low and the big ginger cat sat under the bird feeder. The rush and turns of the winter rain raised a tide of vines on the fences.

We were tricksters on the last card and nothing was in bloom but our stories in the city.

The praying mantis practiced on the lonesome garden path, and the other insects marched higher on the wet stems, higher on the outer leaves, but the sun was not there that morning. The leaves turned with the weight of the crowd and the insects tumbled back to the cold wet earth.

Behind the school a man in a clear plastic shirt served bright green tennis balls to his golden retriever. The retriever chased the green in the rain. The man walked backward and to the sides, as if his retriever had become a golden kite.

We were tricksters and towed our spring and summer kites over the city. Cold reason crashed on the green in the winter rain. We were tricksters out of fashion, out of season, we were the tricksters who mocked the best creations and healed the wounded in a chemical civilization. We were the tricksters who teased the snakes and shouted at the heat on the desert, posed as water ouzel in the mountains, and turned shit into anthropologists. We had four hands and no pockets to hide our stones. The stones carried our stories to the cities, and we heard the bears and the crows rise above the wordies and the dead voices.

We were the last picture on the wanaki cards, the last to be turned and the last connection to the stones and tribal stories in the blood. We were the connection to creation, the last season to the treelines, and we landed our best stories in the cities.

We were the tribal tricksters who created dust mice and invented harmless abusement, appliance bondage, and terminal lectures on deciduous polyvinyl chloride. The trickster turned paradise into a city.

Chivaree was in paradise and she studied her nails on the flea bench near the lake. She was a crossblood wordy, decorated with dead voices, but she was not nervous or hurried, not even when we told her about the fleas who waited on the bench for a ride in her hair to new worlds. The rain had stopped and she was rich, the best reasons not to be in a rush.

Touch the Earth paper cups and fast food containers were on her mind that morning. Chivaree lived on a reservation last summer and two seasons later she was in paradise. She discovered a birch that wanted to be paper, a birch that heard stories and would become the word in the stories, in this case paper cups, from slabs and sawdust. Sometimes the birch heard a rise over the verb, a certain tone of voice, and became a mask, a box of tissue, or even books.

Chivaree was the only one who knew the trickster stories that would inspire the birch to breed paper products. When the birch heard these stories their remains became paper cups and multiplied on their own, a wild parthenogenesis in the birch.

You can understand why she refused to reveal the birch stories to timber companies, but her protection of the birch stories invited severe criticism on the reservation. Some people were convinced that she was no longer tribal, because if she were, she would teach others the stories that would make them rich. So, down on the harmonies of the tribe, she moved her stories and best birch breeders to the city.

The list of new customers and orders in the past month alone was in the thousands, from corporate fast food to the military. The response to the birch cups was sensational, even though people were hesitant to believe that a tree could make cups with nothing more than lost tribal stories. Some wordies had thrown used birch cups together, some were even stacked in rows, and tried many tribal creation stories over the trash but nothing came out of it. The natural practice was close to some idea an advertiser might have proposed, the tree that breeds a natural cup, but in this case the birch turned out nothing but the real, and the real came from stories.

Chivaree was at peace on the flea bench, no one could torment her with riches there. Corporate investors called her at all hours of the night and day with cash offers in the millions for the use of her tribal stories of parthenogenesis in the birch. She reminded the investors that she would rather lose the stories than turn them over to a corporation. You can imagine how much the environmentalists wanted her to teach the world the stories to save the trees, and spare the rivers more pollution. At the same time chemical companies prayed that she would vanish with the tribes, because the birch stories could be an economic disaster if chemicals were not used in paper production.

"So, how did you learn the stories?"

"I don't know, and that's the truth," she said and leaned back on the bench. The fleas waited on her collar and then leaped into her short black hair. "My grandmother had the power of stories, but no one else in the family even speaks the language now."

"You must have heard something?"

"I heard the stories, she was saying something in the language all the time, but it didn't mean anything to me," she said. "Well, not exactly nothing because she could do things with stories, real things."

"What, you mean lust and sex?"

"No, of course not, she could start fires with stories and change the direction of the wind, and everybody knew that she had the power to heal people on the reservation," said Chivaree.

"What about the cups and the birch trees?"

"You won't get me to say the stories."

"Not the stories, but how you first heard the stories."

"I didn't know what she said, so there's nothing to that idea, that some great tribal tradition got hold of me and made me a shaman," she said. "No, nothing like that, she just told these stories and I saw what came of them, and the first one that made a big difference with me was when we were out on the refuge having a picnic and discovered that we forgot the cups, and we only had a big bottle of Coke, so my grandmother just told this little story and suddenly the birch made us cups."

"Just like that?"

"That was it, nothing more to it at the time."

"So, what happened then?"

"Nothing, really, but it was a nice trick to make cups whenever you wanted them," she said. "I asked my grandmother how to talk to the birch and she warned me never to reveal that she had such power, and I didn't until she died."

"The birch forced you to listen, was that it?"

"Not a bad idea, but nobody taught me anything," she said. "I just listened, and in my head practiced the exact sound, the rise and fall of the voice, the way my grandmother spoke to the birch."

"Did it work the first time?"

"Yes, what a surprise," she said. "My grandmother died and the first thing I did after the wake and funeral was go out alone and say the sounds like my grandmother and it worked, the birch made me hundreds of cups the first time out."

"What does it mean?"

"I just say the sounds like my grandmother."

"That's it, no ceremony or anything?"

"No, don't even know what the sounds mean."

"That's truly amazing," we said and threw a stone into the lake. The circle of waves ran over the treeline. "So, why are people so worried on the reservation?"

"That's obvious, you know they just want the money, but the tribe pretends like the stories are some sacred power that would be wasted on me," she said and then sighed on the bench.

"Wasted because you're a crossblood?"

"Right, and because of the language thing."

"So, they can ask traditional leaders."

"That's the trouble, they pretend to be traditional, dance and speak the language some, but no one remembers the stories of the trees, and no wonder they don't hear the trees anymore because the tribal politicians sold every tree they got their hands on in the past century."

"We wanted to be the trickster birch."

"Really, what are you now?"

"We are the birch, would you show us our cups?"

"Very tricky, who are you?"

"Tricksters in the wanaki circle, nothing more."

"Nice try, wiser people than you have tried to trick me out of the birch stories," she said. "My grandmother warned me that the minute the stories are told they lose their power."

"Would you tell the stories if we were birch?"

"Try me, go for the birch."

"You must promise, if we become the birch you will tell us the stories that create the cups," we said and raised our hands. We were worried that if the birch made too many cups we could vanish as tricksters.

We were tricksters on the last turn of the wanaki cards that morning and it was a good time to be a birch tree. So, we told our stories in the blood to the wind in the mountain and we became the birch on the bench near the lake.

"How did you do that?"

"You owe us the stories of the birch."

"You're just like my grandmother, she was so incredible," she said and touched our bare branches. "I would give anything to learn how to do that, you know, to change right in front of people."

"We will show you how to be a birch if you tell us the stories your grandmother knew about the birch, the stories that could turn us into cups," we said and brushed her with our branches.

"No, I could never do that."

"But you promised if we became birch."

"No, my grandmother warned me and she was the only person who ever told the truth, she knew so much and I just can't break my trust and tell anyone."

"But you don't even know what the stories mean."

"I know, and neither does the tribe, and they

think they're so wise and perfect because they don't look like crossbloods, but they are you know, everyone of them is a crossblood, and they know nothing about the power of stories except how much money it might make them."

"Just like you," we said and laughed.

"Don't stay a birch on my account," she said and moved to the end of the bench. "I must be going now, you've been very nice, but I just can't go against my grandmother, she's the only person who has ever made sense to me anywhere, and she's the only one who ever told me stories that never lied about nature."

Chivaree touched our branches at the very moment we turned into trickster bears. She never seemed to be bothered by anything natural, the fleas were dancing in her hair, the birch waited to hear her stories, and when we licked her hand as a bear she swooned and mentioned the stories her grandmother told about luminous bears.

Chivaree never revealed the stories her grandmother told her about the birch, and she was never at peace. She avoided news reporters as best she could without being rude, but when she encouraged the public to throw their birch trash on the roadside she became the focus of much abuse.

"Touch the Earth cups will actually clean up the environment," she announced on a late night talk show. "I know that sounds dumb, but it is true, the birch cups have a natural energy that cares for the roadside in a way that other products do not, so throw birch trash out the window and save the environment."

Touch the Earth was an unusual product to be sure, but no one quite understood what she was talking about, and those who listened were never able to believe that trash was good for the environment. The research scientists in her laboratories had discovered that the birch cups did indeed decompose much more quickly than other products that contained various toxic chemicals.

Chivaree announced that the birch cups became a very good natural mulch on the roadside and in fact created a healthy environment. So, that's what she meant when she encouraged people to throw their trash out the window on the roadside. She printed the pictures of various animals on the cups and used the animals as metaphors, that a cup out the window as trash would get up and run away in a few weeks. Even sooner if it rained. The trashed cups would decompose quicker than a crushed prairie dog.

Politicians search the universe for tics and tacks that might advance their public recognition and reputation, the short bleats and bites are the best, and the idea that some trash is better than other trash was a perfect political bite. For instance, several conservative senators called for a special investigation into the claims of products made by Touch the Earth.

"Something must be done about trash wherever it shows its ugly face," a senator said at the start of the televised hearing. "The public needs no excuse to discard trash at random.

"This woman behind Touch the Earth would turn our nation into trash, perhaps she never cleaned the streets on the Indian reservation where she once lived, but it is a disgrace that she would encourage the desecration of our parks and historical sites with tribal trash, trash, trash."

The senators and their aides were met at the border of the reservation by tribal politicians and police. They wanted firsthand information about the origins of Touch the Earth and the magical claims of the crossblood founder of the company.

"Now then," said the senator, "we are aware that your reservation receives millions of dollars in federal funds for various operations from public health to economic development, so tell me, what is this reservation birch and animals nonsense?"

The senate aide opened a carton of birch cups with animal pictures and threw them out the window as they drove to the tribal headquarters. Network television crews filmed the senator inspecting the trash on the roadside of the reservation. Somehow, the birch cups started eating each other the minute they touched the ground. The cups were gone quicker than the senator could bite the issue on television, so the bite became a new literal pitch.

"God bless this great nation and free enterprise even on a reservation," he said and chewed on the side of a birch cup with the picture of a buffalo. "This very cup that might have provided food to the poor has gone to waste on the roadside."

Chivaree might have lost her shadow if she had not forgotten to bring cups to a picnic with her grandmother. She heard chance and saw creation in the birch. She saw the power of stories and honored those who were tribal healers, and those who died with their stories on the reservation. The healers touched an inner sound in their stories. The sounds of the past hold our memories at a distance, and sight not sound rules the city. Has the city become a sanctuary for those who would create their own tribal stories?

Split Thumbs created his own stories in the city. He was a crossblood elder from the reservation who came to town as a refrigerator repairman and founded the Harmless Abusement and Appliance Bondage Center.

"Machines are no friend of man, woman, or beast, and sometimes they want to rule our worlds," said Split Thumbs. He bought cable television time in the morning to remind the audience that petulant machines and rude appliances, toasters that burn the toast, automobiles that hesitate in traffic, automatic washers that overflow and spread soap on the floor, refrigerators that freeze the milk, hazy television sets, and automatic coffee makers that start in the middle of the night can be disciplined and trained to mind their owners. "Most people think nothing of spending hundreds of dollars to train their dogs, when machines are what need the training."

Thumbs was born with split thumbs and a wild attraction to short and fat blondes. The thumbs were clever, but his need for more than one blonde at a time was trouble. Once a shaman turned him into a woman but that caused even more trouble on the reservation so he was turned back into a man with his stories and sent to the city.

Thumbs lost his riches with blondes more than once. He played poker and was more at home in a casino than anywhere else. He had lived with more than seventeen short fat blondes and each one had to wear a squirrel coat. The coats were his costumes of possession, and he hunted every squirrel that died to make the coats. The elders on the reservation said he hunted squirrels to bag the blondes. Most of his blondes were proud to bear his squirrels, but the fleas never rode the coats. There were seventeen coats near the lake and at least twice a week one brushed the flea bench.

"Are you lonesome this morning because your machines are rude and crude and lazy, do you hate your children and friends, are you in a teeth clenching rage because the trash compactor does not compact, and your disposal will not dispose, and you must touch your own trash so early in the morning?" he asked the television audience.

Thumbs said, "my friends, save your friends

and lovers because what you need now is some advice on how to punish and abuse your appliances to get even, there is nothing more pure than pure vengeance on machines.

"Reach for your telephone now and dial the simple word blondes, spell blondes out on your telephone and we will demonstrate how to handle your special appliance problems, but don't wait, this might be your only chance to get even with your unruly machines before the television set refuses to let you hear this message."

Thumbs never appeared on television without a blonde in a squirrel coat. He wore leather, a feather, beaded moccasins, and practiced a certain accent over his thick false teeth that many viewers thought was a traditional tribal tone of voice. Every time he finished a message he smiled, pinched his fingers in the air, and waved his arms.

"While we wait for the first call to take charge of your machines," he said looking into the camera, "let me remind you that this is the last week to order, at a very special discount, our bondage and abusement instruments, which, as you can see, are whips, hammers, pokers, saws, augers, and other instruments to beat and punish your appliances in the privacy of your own home." The blonde smiled and held up a poker.

"Abusement Center, you're on the air," said Thumbs.

"Yes, listen, I live in a condominium and my toaster refused to hold the bread down this morning, and all I want is one simple slice of toast, is that too much to ask from my toaster?"

"Don't let that toaster join the other machines that want to disrupt your lives, so here is my advice," said Thumbs. "First shut the kitchen door, pull the electrical cord out of the wall, and then take the cord in your hand like this," he said and demonstrated on television. "Then turn the cord, be calm now, you are in complete control of your toaster, around your hand once, the way street fighters wrap chains around their fists, and then raise the toaster from the counter, never mind the crumbs, you can clean that up later, and beat the toaster on the floor until you feel better."

Thumbs told the man to "pull the cord from the toaster, throw it in the trash, and mount the battered toaster somewhere in the house as a reminder to the other machines that you have the power, and then, without delay, this very afternoon, purchase a new toaster at a discount, and here are the list of discount centers.

"So much for abusement this morning, our time has run out," he told the television audience. "Remember, learn to abuse your machines and not your families, take charge of the machines, dominate machines." Thumbs and his blonde waved and the picture dissolved.

We were tricksters on the flea bench near the lake, the last turn of the wanaki cards. The stones in our creation landed in the mountains, near the oceans, and with the tribal sprites on the bench. There were crossbloods and blondes, crows and bears, who carried the fleas in other trickster stories, but the sprites heard stories by the wordies in the city.

Erdupps MacChurbbs was a shaman sprite who ruled three benches on the bay. We heard him in the winter wisteria, posed on an ornamental twist, no higher than our ears, and there he studied the motion of the clouds on the lake. He was wise on the weather, he read books to hear voices on the page, and never told stories until someone asked him to explain one thing or another. So, we asked him to tell a few stories about the triumphs and tragedies of the tribes in the cities.

"Elias Canetti said the 'abandoned earth' was 'overtaxed with words, choking in knowledge, and with no living ear on it to listen into the cold,' and the animals and birds escaped to the city," said the shaman sprite. "Even here, the wordies have overtaxed the cities with too much eye and not enough ears."

"How can we survive the poison rains?"

"Dance in the sun," he said and danced in the wisteria. The sprites were created as tricksters and tribal clowns, and their stories are painted on the stones near the great river. The shaman sprites created their own birds and animals who were heard in his stories. That morning we heard an otter and a crow with him on a branch.

"Smallpox and the rivers are dead," said the otter.

"The wordies lost their connections with the earth," said the crow as she circled the wisteria and the bench. "Wordies have forgotten how to hear and when to surrender to nature and their stories."

Electronic church bells sounded in the distance. The crow bounced on the bench and spread her feathers. "The great river runs past the cities like a sewer, and the wordies hear nothing but dead voices at the university."

"The river is dead and the leaves are down in poison rain," said the otter. She raised her paws on the ocean wind. "The cultures that poison rivers are cultures of evil, and the demons of the chemical underworld must be outwitted to hear our stories on the river."

We raised our noses on the wind and teased the crow on the back of the bench. The crow was a wise trickster, but even tricksters lose their pose in stories. She lost her balance, caught one wing on the rail, and tumbled down into the muck behind the bench. She came back with one of her best stories that last morning of the wanaki game.

"Martin Bear Charme established the Landfill Meditation Reservation on San Francisco Bay. He was a shaman welder who turned to trickster stories, and when he put his mind to the earth he made a fortune hauling and filling wetlands with urban swill and solid waste," said the Crow.

"Bear Charme taught that the wordies

should turn their minds and hearts back to the earth, to meditate on trash, imagine the earth once more and connect the refusers with their refuse," she said and beat her beak on the bench.

"Martin made millions in landfill, more than enough to hire the best lawyers to petition the federal government for recognition as a sovereign nation, the first meditation reservation on a mountain of trash where laws and liens are intuitive, and shamanic flights are basic rights in trickster stories."

The crows heard the landfill stories and hundreds of tricksters circled the bench. The shaman crow cawed and carried on with the other crows in the wisteria. The wordies were covered and no one heard the crows warn them that the rivers and their voices were dead. The fleas on the bench landed on the crows and their stories were carried to their distant relations on the Landfill Meditation Reservation.

We were tricksters on our last chance to warn the wordies that the sheep ranchers would come to the cities to shoot the wolves, the corn farmers would come to shoot crows, and the holiday hunters in the blood would be in town to shoot animals in cold reason.

The cities became our sanctuaries, and we were closer to the natural world in our stories. The wordies lost their stories and honored those creatures who were endangered, but otherwise had no ear for the abandoned earth. We were city tricksters on the road with the best wordies. Not even the brisk wordies heard us as tricksters. We ran as animals, birds, and insects, and told our wanaki stories on the bench. We heard the wise doubts of the wordies, and we set our solace in their dead voices.

# VOICES
January 1980

We must go on, but there is nothing more to be done with our voices in the cities. The tribes are dead, our voices are traced, published, and buried, our voices are dead in the eye of the missionaries. Hold back the promises, hold me back with the bear, send me nothing but sound, sound, sound, to be remembered.

There is no peace, and our best stories must be heard in a trickster war, in the shadows, in a world of chance. Peace is a tragic end, we are lost in peace. Once our stories are written there is no war to hear, to remember our voices and the way we carried on in stones and stories. We must go on, we must go on and be heard over the dead voices.

I would rather be lost at war in the cities than at peace in a tame wilderness. The stories we remember would never survive the peace on federal reservations. Our voices died in the cold hands of the wordies, the missionaries and anthropologists. How else are we to remember the war of stories, and the great migration of our animals to the cities?

There are more bears at the tables in the town than there are on the reservation. Our animals and stories have been hunted down to the last sanctuaries in the cities. The choice is between the chance of tricksters and the drone of cultural pride on reservations. The tribes were invented by these word demons who hunted our animals and buried our voices. The tribes are dead voices. We must go on, but there is nothing to be done.

Leave the wilderness at last to the hunters and wordies, leave him the cultural inventions of his time, leave him on the reservations he invented for the tribes. Leave him there in peace. Remember me with the animals in the mirrors, remember me at war with the wordies, the sound of our new stories in the cities.

We earned nothing from the pious sermons on the traditions of the tribe. Look around, the animals are in the eye and our voices are dead. The peace that ended our war, ended our chance, and that peace comes back to us now in plastic beads and bones. The dance scars are shown with no stories in the ear. We must go on.

The land was discovered by those who were

dead in the heart and unforgiven. The tribes were scarred with inventions, and our stories were removed with the animals. Our voices died on a schedule of civilization, and the war ended in translation.

Our voices are dead and the criers of our deceptions wear plastic chokers, beaded buckles, and imported leathers. Must we celebrate our own assassins and the rise of criminals as our radical leaders?

I died that morning at the end of the wanaki game and there was nothing to be done. Was there a bear in the mirror? Bears are imagined not discovered in fear and rage. Must we be the strangers in the stories of the bear?

I should have known there would be nothing at the end but animals in the mirrors and caged birds, the dead end of the eye, because there was nothing more than that at our creation, and wars of chance in the trickster stories.

We were deceived by the seasons, the great return of nature, the wild patterns of our families, the hounds of sacred ceremonies, and the inventions of the tribes, and with good sense we escaped to the cities with the animals and wounded birds. At last the hunters must hunt each other in their own translations on the reservation. I came alive with the bear in the mirror and died with the tribe in a dead letter translation.

The tribes were created in language, not in the breath of war or the sound and burn of animal ecstasies. Our death would be silence, but the

bear in the mirror was my chance to be remembered in the ear not the eye. The first sight of me
as a bear in the mirror was that wild scent. I
could see me in the sound and stories of the
remembered bear. We were in the ear not the
eye.

I never would have believed that we could
be bears in the cities, as we once were at the old
treelines, if we had not survived in the mirror
and overcome the hunters and assassins of our
stories. We could hear at night the stories that
had been driven with the animals to the cities. We
could hear the sounds that healed the wounded
overnight in the parks. We heard the voices of
creation at the airport, the stories that transformed the waste and garbage into dinner. We
saw the end, the dead voices in the headlines,
and we heard the origin stories of animals and
birds in the cities.

Once we were tracked and translated at the
treeline, we were dead voices in the night, but
now traces of our stories are heard in the cities.
The animals have carried our stories to the cities,
we are their stories, and we are remembered with
them in the mirrors. The mirrors reveal what is
truly there.

I hear in stories and see in the mirror the
bear that others would hunt with fear or watch
in a cage. I am a bear in the mirror. I hear to see,
and stories come to me over the dead voices. I
see in the mirror what others fear to hear. The
past, not death, is our silence, because the past

is the end of the war, the deception of peace. There is no past in the mirror, no past in stones or stories. The past is written and recited not remembered, the past is a separate death, the end of the war and memories. The real past is in the mirror. I am a bear in the mirror, and the bear is my war that heals. We must go on.

I would have been broken on the concrete, dead in the cities, if the bear had not found me in that tabernacle mirror at an antique store. I have always lingered at mirrors and taken pleasure in the reflection of my body in motion, certain turns of my head, the pitch of my arm, and the way the side of my head looks to others. I pretended to be in a film. There were so many mirrors and so many antique stores. I tried to see in the mirror the woman that others must see. Then the bear appeared in the tabernacle. The owner was so startled when she heard we were bears that she reduced the price, but we would have paid any price for our primal union in that mirror.

The bear in the mirror is me, more than manners and poses. The bear is there, the bear is me, the bear is never at peace. We are the stories of the war, the chance in the mirror. We hear each other and we must go on.

I remember the hunter we killed more than a hundred years ago at Bear Island on the Leech Lake Reservation. Now that man haunts me in dreams. My skin falls away, children are skeletons on the island, and the mongrels carry away our skulls from the fire. His relatives brush our shadows at night. His dead voice becomes the silence and loneliness of civilization. He waits on the wind and rushes the seams near me. He follows me on the bus to the airport at night. The beat of my heart remembers his death on the island that spring. The bear crushed the head of that white hunter when he raised his rifle and fired once. The bullet hit me in the shoulder, tore the flesh but not my bones. There is no way to escape the silence of his death but in the mirror.

The tabernacle mirror heard me as the bear, and the bear remembers the death of a hunter and the end of civilization. There are no separations in the mirror, the war goes on in our stories. The wanaki game is our war with the wordies and the peace of their dead voices. Our seasons are the same at last. We must go on.

BAGESE
February 1992

Bagese Bear vanished with the turn of the trickster card at the end of the wanaki game. She has never been seen since then, not at the treelines on the reservation or at Lake Merritt. The ivy at the window, the stone on the table, and mold shadows were left behind in her garden apartment, but nothing more. The tabernacle mirror was gone with the last traces of our stories.

I remembered many years later that she had bought that tabernacle mirror at an antique store near the lake. My hunch was right, the mirror was there. The owner said the tabernacle had been returned to the store with no explanation. She mounted the mirror on an easel near the entrance and waited for the owner to return.

Some months later she removed it to the back of the store because several children saw a bear in the mirror and were frightened. One child screamed in terror and was hurt running from the store. Two men ran into traffic on the busy street to escape the bear. No one else could see the bear, but the owner was concerned and covered the mirror in the back room.

I raised the cloth cover and saw the bear in the tabernacle. I cried at the sight of my old friend who taught me to see the real world in stories. The owner of the antique store was obliged to hear my stories about the woman who became a bear. She was amused at first, but soon she was too worried to listen, terrified that a demon bear would leap from the tabernacle and claim the other mirrors in the store. She reminded me that nature was at peace in her heart and told me to remove the tabernacle. That mirror is with me now because of the bear stories. Once or twice a year some visitor might see the shadow of a bear in the mirror. Those who hear the bear are there to hear the stories of the old woman.

Bagese became a bear, and at last she became a picture of a bear. She sent me a copper dish with several figures marked on the wide circle. The copper was once a sacred record of the woodland tribe. The first figure was the trickster at creation, and the other figures were tribal generations at the great river. Then there was a man with a high hat on the circle. He was taller than the others and must have been the first white man to reach the tribe, an explorer at the source of the great river no doubt.

The last figure was a new mark on the copper, the incised outline of a bear. The bear was framed with rosettes in the corners. There, she tried to represent the tabernacle mirror. At last the bear in the cities was heard in sacred tribal histories.

Bagese must have remembered my promise and sent that copper record to me. I telephoned her uncle on the reservation, but he had not seen her for more than twenty years. Sucker was amused that she became a bear. He told me that her name means a tribal dish game in translation, and the last he heard she was out on the desert with the bear women. Who else would know about that copper and the bear in the mirror?

I waited a few more years and then decided that the stories she told me must be published. She warned me otherwise, but she made the first record and published the first mark for the eye not the ear. The figure of the bear on the copper dish would have been silent if we had not published the stories she remembered and told to me. I know she would say that the mark of the bear was her imagination, that the picture must be heard, the same argument we had over the wanaki pictures, but the mark on the copper was incised as a record of tribal creation and stories. That copper has become a written record of the return of the bear.

Bagese would pound me on the head if she

heard me say that the real trouble with published stories is where our troubles ought to be, because dead voices have no troubles. The published stories over those we hear are not more trouble than the earth over our bodies, cold water over a hot red stone, a cage to hold the wounded crows, or so it seems in most translations. The stories of the bear survived the hunters, and the bear in the mirror endures the published stories.

Bagese, these published stories are the same as the wanaki pictures and the stones that you placed in your apartment to remember the earth, the traces of birds and animals near the lake. I am with you in the mirror, and hold a stone in my pocket, the stone you left for me on the table, to remember your stories. We must go on.